Official
Cambridge
Exam
Preparation

COMPLETE

KEY
for Schools

Workbook
without answers

T0306620

A2

WITH AUDIO
DOWNLOAD

Sue Elliott and
Emma Heyderman

Cambridge University Press
www.cambridge.org/elt

Cambridge Assessment English
www.cambridgeenglish.org

Information on this title: www.cambridge.org/9781108539401

© Cambridge University Press and UCLES 2019

First published 2013

20 19 18 17

Printed in Italy by L.E.G.O. S.p.A.

A catalogue record for this publication is available from the British Library

ISBN 978-1-108-53940-1 Workbook without answers with Audio Download

Contents

1 Hi, how are you?

Listening Part 1

Look carefully at the question and the pictures before each recording starts.

Exam advice

1 For each question, choose the correct answer.

1 Where is Sarah's brother?

A   B   C

2 How much were Jon's baseball boots?

A   B   C

3 Which picture shows Marta's brother and sister?

A   B   C

4 What do Holly and her friends usually do on Saturdays?

A   B   C

5 Which person in Kasia's family has a birthday at the weekend?

A   B   C

Grammar
Present simple

1 Complete the sentences with the correct form of *do*.

1 We ....*don't*........ go to school on Saturdays. It's the weekend.
2 Where .... you live?
3 Tom and Ben .... go to the cinema very often, maybe three times a year.
4 Which company .... your dad work for?
5 My sister .... like shopping. She prefers doing sport.
6 What time .... I need to get up tomorrow?
7 I like football, but I .... really like tennis.
8 What .... your little brother prefer, apples or bananas?

2 Complete the blog with the correct form of the verb in the brackets.

My name's Chloe and I
(1) ....*live*.... (live) in Manchester with my mum and younger sister. My grandma lives with us, too.
I (2) .... (get up) at 7.30 every day because I (3) .... (be) still at school. But I (4) .... (not live) far from my school, so I can walk there in a few minutes. My mum's name (5) .... (be) Joanna and she (6) .... (teach) at a college. I usually (7) .... (have) my lunch at school, but my mum (8) .... (have) her lunch at a café near her college. She (9) .... (not teach) every afternoon because her students sometimes (10) .... (finish) at lunchtime. But when she's at college all day, she usually (11) .... (drive) home. Then in the evening Mum (12) .... (watch) TV and I (13) .... (play) my guitar. I use my headphones so that it (14) .... (not be) too loud for my grandma!

3 Chloe's English teacher is asking her some questions. Complete the questions and answers. Use the correct form of *be* or *do*.

1 ....*Do*.... you get up early every day?
Yes, *I do* .
2 ....*Is*.... your sister at school today?
Yes, *she is* .
3 .... you hungry?
No, ...
4 .... your mum have lunch at work?
No, ...
5 .... it cold outside today?
No, ...
6 .... you like music?
Yes, ...

Adverbs of frequency

4 Circle the correct adverbs.

1 I get up at 7 o'clock, but not at the weekends! I (usually)/ sometimes get up at 7 o'clock.
2 I play football every Saturday morning. I *never / always* play football on Saturdays.
3 I go to the sports centre quite a lot – about three times a week. I *sometimes / often* go to the sports centre during the week.
4 Every day I ask my big brother to drive me to school. I *sometimes / always* ask my big brother to drive me to school.
5 My dad gives me chocolate about once a week. My dad *usually / sometimes* gives me chocolate.
6 My friend Keira doesn't go into town – she doesn't like it. I *usually / never* see Keira in the town centre.

5 ⊙ Exam candidates often make mistakes with the position of adverbs of frequency. Correct the mistakes in each of these sentences.

1 You are ~~welcome always~~ in my home. *always welcome*
2 I don't watch often TV. ....
3 I like it because I always can buy new games. ....
4 The weather is very beautiful and I stay often on the beach. ....
5 The festival has sometimes funfairs. ....
6 I don't go usually to school at 6 am. ....

Vocabulary
Family members

1 Put the letters in the right order to make words about family members.

1 steris   *sister*
2 bahnsud   ....
3 cleun   ....
4 nicsou   ....
5 madragn   ....
6 grudateh ....
7 rohbret   ....
8 naiteu   ....

Reading Part 2

Underline the most important information in each question, and then look carefully to find it in the texts.

1 For each question, choose the correct answer.

		Mark	Ryan	Ashley
1	Who usually watches a new film?	A	B	C
2	Who stays at home in the evenings?	A	B	C
3	Who lives close to another family member?	A	B	C
4	Who gets up later than usual some mornings?	A	B	C
5	Who really enjoys doing some sport?	A	B	C
6	Who doesn't like going shopping?	A	B	C
7	Who sees his friends in town?	A	B	C

Three boys talk about how they spend their Saturdays.

Mark

I usually get up at 7 am on school days, but on Saturdays I stay in bed until 10 am. It's great! Then in the afternoon, my parents come to watch me play football. It's often really cold, so it's not much fun — but Mum always brings hot drinks! In the evenings, my two brothers are always in town with friends. My cousin Josh comes to my house and we watch a film together. It's usually an old one that we both enjoy.

Ryan

I live with my dad and younger sister. Dad takes us swimming in the morning, so I need to get up early. Then in the afternoon we go to the supermarket in town to buy food. That's a bit boring, but I know he can't do it himself. He usually works on Saturday evenings, so my sister and I go to my auntie's house. It's on the same street as our house. We all sit and watch fantastic old movies together — it's cool!

Ashley

I have basketball practice at 9 am, so I get up at the same time as a school day — I hate that! But I love playing the game. In the afternoons, I meet some of my classmates at the shopping centre in town. We buy a few things, and then go and see one of the latest movies. In the evenings, we sometimes drive to my grandma's. It takes a long time to get there, but we love visiting her.

Writing Part 6

Underline what you must include in your answer. When you've finished, check that you have included the three points in your writing.

1 Read this exam task. <u>Underline</u> the questions.

> **From:** Jade
>
> **To:** Zoe
>
> I'm glad that you can come to town with me on Saturday. What time shall we go? How shall we get there? What do you want to do in town?

2 Look at Zoe's email and answer the questions.

> **From:** Zoe
>
> **To:** Jade
>
> Hi Jade,
>
> Let's go into town at 2 o'clock. We can go on the bus. We can go shopping, and then we can see a film.
>
> See you on Saturday!
>
> Zoe

1 How does Zoe begin and finish her email to Jade?

....

2 Does she answer all three questions? Is her email long enough?

....

3 Read the email from your English friend, Alex.

> **From:** Alex
>
> **To:**
>
> Thanks for asking me to come to your house on Saturday. What time shall I come? Where do you live? What shall we do together?

**Write an email to Alex and answer the questions.
Write 25 words or more.**

1 Vocabulary extra

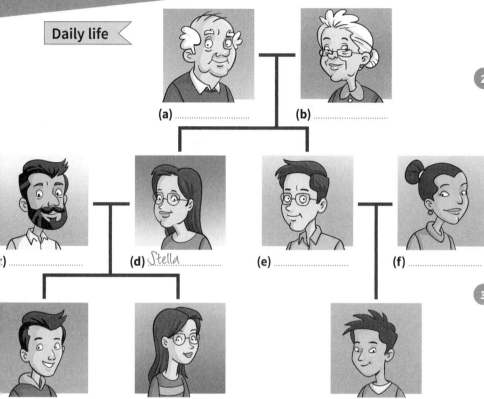

(a) .... (b) ....

) .... (d) *Stella* .... (e) .... (f) ....

) .... (h) .... (i) ....

1a **Label the people in the family tree using the sentences below.**

1 Maria is Stella's daughter.
2 Michael is Stella's brother.
3 Henry is Michael's father.
4 Agnes is Henry's wife.
5 Ben is Maria's cousin.
6 Connie is Maria's auntie.
7 Richard is Ben's uncle.
8 Dan is Richard's son.

1b **Look at the family tree again and complete the sentences.**

1 Agnes is Dan's ......*grandma*...... .
2 Richard is Stella's ....
3 Michael is Dan's ....
4 Connie is Michael's ....
5 Ben is Connie's ....
6 Maria is Dan's ....
7 Maria is Richard's ....
8 Ben is Dan's ....

2 **Match the verbs 1–10 to the nouns a–j.**

1	have	a	an exam
2	brush	b	your clothes
3	take	c	a car
4	do	d	a shower
5	go	e	your teeth
6	put on	f	basketball
7	drive	g	shopping
8	get on	h	a bus
9	watch	i	a film
10	play	j	the washing-up

3 **Complete the crossword using the clues below.**

Across

1 What number do you get if you add 9 + 9?
3 What number comes after two?
4 How many players are there in a football team?
6 How many days are there in two weeks?
7 What is 10 x 4?

Down

2 How many months are there in a year?
5 How many days are there in April, June and September in total?

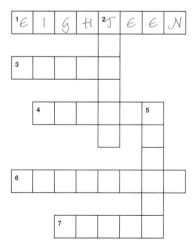

2 We're going home

Listening Part 3

Exam advice

Try to answer each question the first time you listen, and then check your answers the second time you listen.

1 For each question, choose the correct answer. You will hear Jake and his sister Ava talking about their new house.

1 What does Jake like about their new house?
- **A** The garden is tidy.
- **B** The kitchen is big.
- **C** The living room is warm.

2 Ava likes where the house is because
- **A** she can see the park from her window.
- **B** she can go to the library to study.
- **C** she can get to the river easily.

3 Jake says their house is unusual because
- **A** it has white walls.
- **B** it has a red roof.
- **C** it's made of wood.

4 What does Ava still want to buy for her room?
- **A** a comfortable chair
- **B** an alarm clock
- **C** a bookshelf

5 How do they decide to get to school every day?
- **A** by bike
- **B** on foot
- **C** by car

Grammar
Present continuous

1 Complete the sentences with the correct form of the verbs.

> rain   ride   sleep   wash   ~~work~~   write

1 My dad's got the day off, so he ....*isn't working*........... today.
2 The baby .... upstairs, so please be quiet.
3 We can go to the park because it .... any more.
4 Ryan and Tom .... their hands before lunch.
5 Harry .... his own bike. That one is his brother's.
6 I .... a letter to my uncle. It's his birthday soon.

2 ⊙ **Exam candidates often make mistakes with present continuous forms. Correct the mistakes in each of these sentences.**

1 I can't play football because I'm ~~writting~~ a story. ....*writing*.......
2 Jack isn't comming to my party because he's sick. ....
3 We're not goeing to school by bus today. ....
4 Is Sam listening to rock music on his computer? ....
5 We're at the beach and my brother's swiming. ....
6 Are you enjoing that book you're reading? ....

have got

3 Complete the text with the correct form of *have got*.

Our new flat is great! I (1) ....*have got*.......... my own room – I don't share with my brother now! I like my room because it (2) .... a big window. My older brother's room is next door. He (3) .... a lot of things in his room. There's a comfortable chair and a big desk but he (4) .... a TV. My parents (5) .... the biggest bedroom in the flat. In our last home they had a bedroom with a shower, but they (6) .... one in this place. (7) .... you .... your own room in your home?

4 ⊙ Exam candidates often make mistakes with *have got*. Add *got* in the correct places in the sentences.

1 I'm selling my old tablet because I've got a new one.
  ^

2 Have you a special dress to wear for the party?

3 We haven't a pet in our family.

4 I've some friends who play in a rock band.

5 Olivia has a lot of presents for her birthday.

6 Have you any money in your bag?

Reading Part 1

1 For each question, choose the correct answer.

1

> Megan
> I'm at home today – I'm painting the walls of my room green! Come and tell me what you think.
> Max

What does Max want Megan to do?

A choose a colour for him to paint his room

B help him paint his room a different colour

C give him her opinion about the colour of his room

2

> End-of-term school party!
>
> Classroom 3B   All students welcome
> Friday 17th   Bring food!
> Mrs Harrison

A To attend this party, you need to be a student from Classroom 3B.

B Mrs Harrison will bring something to the party for students to eat.

C Everyone at the school is invited to the party on the 17th.

3

> Mum,
> I've left my sports kit at home – and I'm playing hockey today!
> Could you bring it to school and leave it at reception, please? Thanks!
> Karl

Karl wants his mum to

A take something he's forgotten to school.

B meet him at the school reception with his sports kit.

C come to his school to watch him play hockey.

4

> MUSIC CLUB STARTING AGAIN SOON
> First meeting next Thurs 4 pm.
> Come and join us!

A You have to join the club before you can go to the first meeting.

B Anyone can go along to the music club next Thursday.

C There is a new music club beginning soon that you can attend.

5

> Sarah,
> My dad's working on Saturday evening, so he can't come and collect us from Ben's party. Could your dad please come instead, at 11 pm?
> Amy

A Amy is checking what time Ben's party finishes on Saturday.

B Amy wants to know if Sarah's dad can give them a lift home on Saturday.

C Amy is asking Sarah to travel back from the party with her on Saturday.

6

> Don't keep this soup in the fridge for more than two days after opening it.

A If you open this soup, only keep it in the fridge for two days.

B You must open and eat this soup in the next two days.

C Put this soup in the fridge as soon as you open it.

Vocabulary
Rooms

1 Put the letters in the right order to make the names of things you might find in the home.

1 rtmaoboh ....bathroom.......
2 regaga ....
3 sirtas ....
4 cenkith ....
5 niwdwo ....
6 orofl ....
7 morbdeo ....
8 dregan ....
9 flit ....
10 migsinmw lopo ....

Furniture

2 Match the objects 1–6 with the information a–f.

1 bookshelf   **a** You sit on this.
   b This is on the floor of a room.
2 carpet
   c You can do your homework on this.
3 chair
   d These are on each side of your window.
4 desk
   e You switch this on to see more clearly.
5 lamp
   f You put your books on this in your room.
6 curtains

Writing Part 7

What things can you see in each picture? Try to include all of them in your story.

Exam advice

1 Find the things in the three pictures. Then use the words in your story.

boxes   boy   carry   dog   empty   furniture   grass
house   lorry   outside   parents   pizza   sit   sofa

2 Look at the three pictures.
Write the story shown in the pictures.
Write 35 words or more.

At home

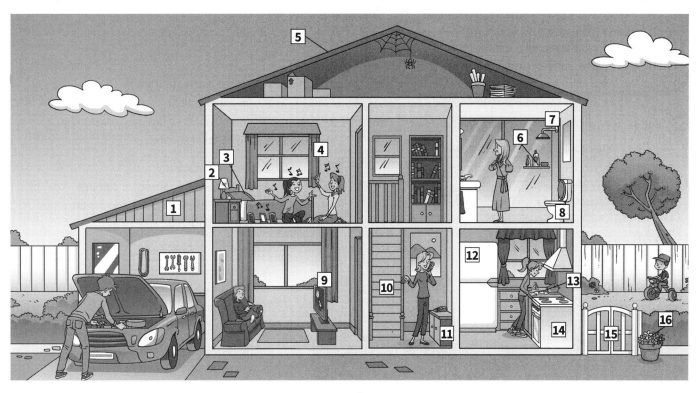

1a Complete the sentences with a correct form of the verbs from the box and names of rooms.

> brush ~~cook~~ listen repair
> ride watch talk

1 I'm __cooking__ in the __kitchen__ . I'm making lunch.
2 Jay is .... TV on the sofa in the ....
3 Maria and Amy are .... to music upstairs. They're in their ....
4 Dad is .... the car. He's outside, in front of the ....
5 Grandma is .... her hair in the ....
6 Jack is .... his new bike outside in the ....
7 Mum is .... to her friend on the phone in the ....

1b Match the words with 1–16 in the picture.

cooker	_14_	cupboard	....
curtains	....	flowers	....
fridge	....	garage	....
gate	....	lamp	....
plate	....	pillow	....
roof	....	shelf	....
shower	....	stairs	....
toilet	....	TV	....

2 Find the odd one out.

1 shower (pillow) toilet towel
2 flowers carpet trees grass
3 bedroom living room kitchen furniture
4 computer TV chair lamp
5 blanket cooker lamp bed
6 door gate bookshelf window
7 apartment garage house flat

3 Dinner time

Reading Part 3

Read the text very carefully to find your answer. <u>Underline</u> the parts of the text where the answer comes from.

Exam advice

1 For each question, choose the correct answer.

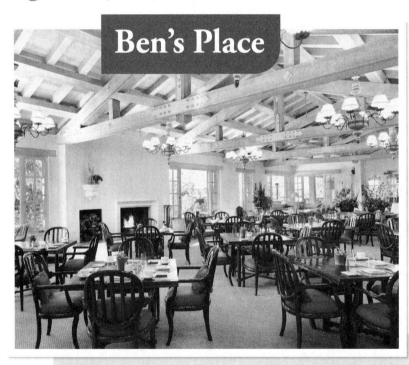

Ben's Place

1 Anna and her parents like the restaurant because
 A it's good for family birthdays.
 B it's not usually full.
 C it isn't very expensive.

2 Anna says the restaurant is
 A on a busy road.
 B near a fast food café.
 C in the town square.

3 Inside the restaurant
 A the walls are a variety of colours.
 B someone is always playing music.
 C the staff are really friendly.

4 When Anna gets the menu, she
 A can't decide what to order.
 B doesn't usually know many dishes on it.
 C has to ask her dad to choose for her.

5 What does Anna say about the food she has at the restaurant?
 A It's as good as her dad's cooking.
 B She wants to try making the dishes herself.
 C The curries are the best things there.

Anna Kriss writes about her favourite restaurant

Do you have a favourite restaurant that you go to with your family? I do! It's called Ben's Place, a new restaurant in my town. Not many people know about it yet, so it's never really busy – which is why we enjoy eating there. It costs more than some restaurants, but the food's good. I'm hoping to go there for my next birthday!

Ben's Place is easy to find, but it's not in the town square, with all the other restaurants and fast food cafés. Instead, it's on a road going out of town, which always has lots of cars driving along it. But you can usually find somewhere to park outside.

When you go into the restaurant, a waiter always comes to say hello, and another one chats to you as you walk to your table. The restaurant looks great inside, with lovely yellow walls. And there's often someone playing the piano, which is nice.

There are wonderful dishes on the menu. Lots of them are things we eat at home. But when I'm at the restaurant, I never know which to have – they all sound good! Dad tries to give me advice, but I prefer to choose for myself.

Everything's delicious, especially the soups and the curries. My dad's a good cook, so I'm hoping one day soon he'll teach me to cook what we have at the restaurant. But my dishes will never be as good as the ones at Ben's Place!

Vocabulary
Food phrases

1 Look at the pictures. Match the containers 1–8 with the food and drink a–h.

1 a bottle of   a beans
2 a bowl of   b chocolates
3 a can of   c chips
4 a cup of   d cheese
5 a glass of   e orange juice
6 a plate of   f tea
7 a piece of   g soup
8 a box of   h mineral water

2 Cross out the word which is not correct.

1 a bowl / ~~slice~~ / box of cereal
2 a glass / box / bottle of milk
3 a can / slice / plate of pizza
4 a piece / slice / glass of toast
5 a bag / bottle / bowl of apples
6 a piece / can / glass of lemonade
7 a box / plate / cup of biscuits

School lunches

3 Complete the school café menu.

School café menu
1 b u r g ℓ r
2 c h … s …
   s … n d w … c h … s
3 f … s h and c h … p s
4 c h … c k … n s … l … d
5 … p p l … s
6 b … n … n … s
7 … c … c r … … m
8 … r … n g … j … … c …
9 l … m … n … d …

Listening Part 2

Look carefully at the questions before the recording starts. Think about what kind of information you need.

Exam advice

1 For each question, write the correct answer in the gap. Write one word or a number or a date or a time. You will hear a woman on the radio talking about a festival.

 04

International Festival

Type of festival: .... *food* ....
Date: (1) ....
Place: (2) .... Park
Time festival opens: (3) .... pm
How many visitors will get free gift: (4) ....
Visitors can make: (5) ....

Grammar

Countable and uncountable nouns

1 What's in the shopping basket? Complete the sentences with *is / isn't / are / aren't + a / an / some / any*.

1 There .... *are some* .... apples.
2 There .... cheese.
3 There .... grapes.
4 There .... eggs.
5 There .... onion.
6 There .... lemonade.
7 There .... orange juice.
8 There .... carrot.

How much / many; a few, a little, a lot of

2 Complete the questions with *How much* or *How many*. Then circle the correct answer.

1 *How many* sweets would you like?
   (A lot.) / *None*. I love them!
2 .... bananas do you eat in a week?
   Only a few. / Only a little. One or two, maybe.
3 .... pasta would you like?
   Just a few, / Just a little, please. I'm not very hungry.
4 .... ice cream would you like?
   A lot, / A little, please. It's my favourite!
5 .... bread have we got?
   Only a few. / Only a little. We need to buy some.
6 .... oranges are you going to buy?
   A lot. / None. I haven't got any money in my bag.

3 ⦿ Exam candidates often make mistakes with *how much / how many, a few / a little / a lot* and *a / any / some*. Circle the correct answer.

1 *(How much)/ How many* sugar do you want?
2 Don't use *a lot of / a little of* salt.
3 We've still got *a few / a little* carrots in the kitchen.
4 *How much / How many* fruit do you eat a day?
5 Is there *a / any* butter in the fridge?
6 Would you like *some / a* bread?

Reading Part 5

Read the whole email first before you start writing.

Exam advice

1 Complete these emails. Write ONE word for each space.

From: Markus
To: Josh

Hi Josh,

How (0) .... *are* .... you? My name's Markus and I live in (1) .... north of Germany, in Hamburg. I live with my parents and older brother. My favourite hobby is making pizza! I always make a big one (2) .... my friends to eat when they come to my house.

(3) .... you like to be my penfriend? I hope so! Write and tell (4) .... all about yourself!

Markus

From: Josh
To: Markus

Hi Markus,

I'd love to be (5) .... penfriend! I live in Italy and I go to school every day. I enjoy cooking, too! I can send you some great pizza recipes (6) .... you want!

Write soon,

Josh

3 Vocabulary extra

Food

1 Write the names of the items in the picture.

1 _tomatoes_
2 ....
3 ....
4 ....
5 ....
6 ....
7 ....
8 ....

2 Put these items into the correct box.

> ~~bananas~~ burgers carrots chicken coffee grapes
> lemons milk onions potatoes steak tea

Fruit	Vegetables
bananas,	

Meat	Drinks

3 Circle the correct words.

1 a (glass) / slice of water
2 a piece / box of chocolates
3 a bottle / piece of meat
4 a slice / box of cheese
5 a bowl / can of cereal

4 Complete the sentences with the correct form of a word from the box.

> bowl box cake ~~egg~~ fork
> knife lunch plate
> sandwich tomato

1 To make an omelette, you need a few _eggs_ .
2 We need some more .... for people to cut their food with.
3 You can put food on these .... when you serve it to people.
4 Have we got enough .... to put the soup in?
5 We usually have our .... in the middle of the day.
6 Let's make some .... for the picnic with this bread and cheese.
7 You can use a .... to put food into your mouth.
8 My mum always bakes me a special .... for my birthday.
9 Look! We've got two .... of chocolates to eat during the film!
10 Have we got any .... to put on top of the pizza?

4 I'm shopping!

Listening Part 5

> You will hear information about each person in the same order as the list.

Exam advice

1 For each question, choose the correct answer.
You will hear Tom talking to a friend about going shopping with his family. What did each person buy?

People		Things they bought
0 Tom	*C*	**A** bag
1 sister	....	**B** dress
2 dad	....	**C** jeans
3 mum	....	**D** shirt
4 brother	....	**E** shoes
5 grandma	....	**F** suit
		G T-shirt
		H watch

Grammar
Present continuous and present simple

1 Circle the correct words to complete these sentences.

1 Jack *plays* / is playing football every weekend.
2 What *do you do* / *are you doing* at the moment?
3 We *are having* / *have* three bedrooms in our house.
4 My sister *watches* / *is watching* a fashion show on TV this evening.
5 Mum and Dad *want* / *are wanting* a cup of tea – they've just come home.
6 Tom is outside the cinema. He *is waiting* / *waits* for his dad to collect him.
7 I'm talking to my dog, but he *doesn't understand* / *isn't understanding* me.
8 *Do you know* / *Are you knowing* where I can buy some cool trainers?

2 Complete the text with the verbs in brackets. Use the present simple or the present continuous.

At the moment (1) ___I'm sitting___ (sit) in the living room at home. My brother and I (2) _____ (play) computer games and we (3) _____ (have) a snack. We always (4) _____ (play) our favourite games when we (5) _____ (come) home from school. Mum's in the kitchen – she (6) _____ (cook) our supper tonight. She (7) _____ (not cook) every evening – that's usually Dad's job because she (8) _____ (get) home from work late. But she had a day off today. Dad (9) _____ (travel) home from work now. He'll be home soon.

3 ⊙ Exam candidates often make mistakes with the present simple and present continuous. Correct the mistakes in each of these sentences.

1 ~~She's liking~~ the clothes she bought.
she likes

2 I am wanting to read that book, too.
....

3 I not needing it because I have a new living room.
....

4 I'm having lunch at 12.30 every day.
....

5 My favourite films are action films. I'm loving them.
....

6 Jack isn't liking the jeans he got – they're very big.
....

7 Are you knowing my friend John?
....

too and *enough*

4 Look at the pictures and complete the sentences about Ben. Use *too / enough* and the adjectives from the box.

> big heavy ~~long~~ old
> ~~short~~ small strong young

1 Ben can't wear these trousers because they are
.... *too short* ....

Ben can't wear these trousers because they aren't
.... *long enough* ....

2 Ben can't join the team because he's
....

Ben can't join the team because he isn't
....

3 The bag is .... for Ben to carry.
Ben isn't .... to carry the bag.

4 The cake was .... for three people.
The cake wasn't .... for three people.

Reading Part 4

Choose the word that goes with what's before and after the gap.

Exam advice

1 Read the article about a teenager who makes her own clothes. For each question, choose the correct answer.

Rowena Davis

Rowena Davis is 15 years old and lives in London. Her **(1)** .... thing to do there is to look around the clothes shops, because she's very **(2)** .... in fashion. She's brilliant at drawing, and she **(3)** .... drawing pictures of different clothes to drawing people or places. She **(4)** .... knows how to make some of the clothes that she draws! **(5)** .... month she decided to enter a fashion competition in a magazine with one of the dresses she made – and she won! 'I made a beautiful party dress – and the judges loved it!' says Becky. 'When I'm older, I'd like to have a **(6)** .... making clothes for famous people, and earn lots of money. That would be fantastic!'

1	**A** important	**B** favourite	**C** best
2	**A** interested	**B** excited	**C** good
3	**A** wants	**B** decides	**C** prefers
4	**A** yet	**B** even	**C** quite
5	**A** Last	**B** Next	**C** Past
6	**A** course	**B** work	**C** job

4

Vocabulary
Shops

1 **Put the letters in the right order to find the names of shops.**

1 You can buy clothes and food, and it's often outside.
kremat ...._market_............

2 This big shop sells everything. It's usually cheap!
trempusarke ....

3 This sells all kinds of things, like good clothes and shoes – but it can be very expensive.
predemtant osret ....

4 Go here if you need a dictionary for your studies. They'll have the one you need.
skopboho ....

5 This place sells medicines and things for your health.
shimect ....

Adjectives

2 **Look at the pictures and complete the phrases using the words from the box.**

| cheap clean dark ~~dirty~~ expensive large light |
| long new old small short |

1 a ...._dirty_....... T-shirt
a .... T-shirt

2 .... boots
.... boots

3 a .... dress
a .... dress

4 a .... sweater
a .... sweater

5 .... trainers
.... trainers

6 a .... jacket
a .... jacket

Writing Part 7

When you have finished your writing, spend a few minutes checking your work.
Make sure you've written complete sentences.

Exam advice

1 **Look at the following text. Put full stops or capital letters into the text. There are four sentences.**

tom goes into a clothes shop because he wants to buy a new sweater he finds a nice one that he likes he tries on the sweater, but it's too small he's very unhappy

2 **Look at the three pictures. Write the story shown in the pictures. Write 35 words or more.**

4 Vocabulary extra

Clothes adjectives

1 Look at the people. Complete the descriptions, using the words from the box.

A   B   C

> bag   belt   boots   dress   hat   jacket   jeans
> shirt   suit   sunglasses   ~~sweater~~   tie   trainers
> umbrella   watch

A Jamie is wearing a dark (1) ...._sweater_........ and a pair of light blue (2) .... He's wearing a big pair of (3) .... and a black (4) .... He's wearing (5) .... because it's sunny.

B Saskia is wearing a pretty (6) .... with a black (7) .... and a long (8) .... She's wearing white (9) .... , and she's carrying a small (10) ....

C Mr Bell is wearing a dark (11) .... , a white (12) .... and a blue and red (13) .... He's wearing an expensive silver (14) .... and he's carrying a large (15) ....

2 In a big store, which department would you go to for the following things?

1	necklace	a	jewellery
2	football shorts	b	women's clothes
3	boots	c	sports clothes
4	skirt	d	shoes
5	swimming costume	e	men's clothes
6	ring		
7	dress		
8	tie		

3 Look at the verbs below. Then complete the sentences with the verbs.

> **put on** clothes in the morning
> **take off** clothes to go to bed
> **try on** clothes in a shop before buying them
> **change out** of old jeans and **change into** something nice for a party

1 Excuse me, could I ...._try on_.......... this T-shirt?

2 My family and I are going out to dinner tonight, so I need to .... my school clothes and .... a nice dress before I go.

3 I'm too hot. I need to .... this thick sweater.

4 I should .... my coat – it's cold tonight.

4 Complete the sentences with the adjectives in the box.

> crowded   dark   dirty   ~~heavy~~   high   low

1 I can't carry these shopping bags – they're really ...._heavy_.......... .

2 The bus into town is sometimes so .... that we can't get on it.

3 I don't really like the colour of this T-shirt – it's too .... I'd prefer a lighter one.

4 That sports shop has very .... prices. Let's look inside!

5 My football shirt is .... , so I need to wash it.

6 The sweaters are on a .... shelf, so I can't get them. Could you help me, please?

5 It's my favourite sport!

Exam advice

Read the text carefully, then <u>underline</u> the parts that give you the answers.

1 For each question, choose the correct answer.

Running and blogging!
by Holly Parsons

Everyone in my family enjoys running – including me! But it's sometimes hard for me to find someone to run with. My brother and I sometimes run together, but he's much faster than me. And my dad's too busy to come at the moment. So my best running partner these days is my cousin Mandy. We go almost every day – it's great! We don't go running when it's raining, but I still want to keep fit on those days, so I go to the gym, or I play badminton with Mum. And sometimes I swim in the local pool. That's what I like the most!

I also write a blog about running. I began writing it because I liked writing posts about where I go running, how I feel when I run, and the kinds of kit I like wearing. Now lots of people follow my blog, and they give me great advice! Some even say they started running after reading my blog, so that's great!

Of course, not all my friends are interested in running, so I don't ask them to come with me. But they can see it's really important to me, and they always want to know about my latest runs, so that's nice.

I'd like to improve my running so I can enter more races. I've done some local races, but I've never won anything – but that doesn't matter. I'd really like to try a 25 km race soon. Everyone says it's hard – but we'll see!

1 Who does Holly usually go running with?
- **A** her cousin
- **B** her father
- **C** her brother

2 What is Holly's favourite way to keep fit when the weather's bad?
- **A** going to the gym
- **B** swimming
- **C** playing badminton

3 Why did Holly start writing a blog about running?
- **A** to share her experiences of running
- **B** to give advice to other runners
- **C** to help other teenagers to start running

4 Holly says that her friends
- **A** sometimes join her when she goes running.
- **B** like asking her about her running.
- **C** don't really understand why she runs.

5 What does Holly want to do next?
- **A** win a competition
- **B** enter her first competition
- **C** run in a difficult competition

Comparatives and superlatives

1a Fill in the table with the correct comparative and superlative forms.

	adjective	comparative	superlative
1	big	bigger	the biggest
2	heavy		
3	hard		
4	exciting		
5	cheap		
6	expensive		
7	good		
8	bad		

1b Now complete the sentences with the correct form of the adjectives from Exercise 1a.

1   A tennis ball is ...._heavier_........ than a table tennis ball – that's very light.

2   This sports centre is .... I've ever been to – it costs a lot to get in.

3   Jon is .... at basketball than me. He's in the school team and I'm not!

4   I think football is .... to play than other sports because there are lots of rules.

5   I bought .... racket in the shop because I didn't have much money.

6   Snowboarding is much .... than skating – that's boring!

Prepositions of time *at, in, on*

2 Write *at, in* or *on* where necessary. Some words don't need a preposition.

1   ....—........ tomorrow

2   ...._on_........ Saturday

3   .... summer

4   .... night

5   .... 10.30 pm

6   2010

7   .... yesterday

8   .... Friday afternoon

9   .... the weekend

10 .... next week

3 ◉ Exam candidates often make mistakes with prepositions of time. Correct the mistakes in each of these sentences.

1   We will go on the 5th October ~~at the evening~~ .
     in the evening ....

2   I'm free in Monday afternoon.
     ....

3   I'm arriving 6.30 pm.
     ....

4   We can meet in 5 o'clock.
     ....

5   I had a nice time in my birthday.
     ....

6   At the first day, you should take a notebook.
     ....

Look carefully at each question and the options A, B and C before the recording starts.

Exam advice

06

1 For each question, choose the correct answer.

1   You will hear a boy talking to his friend about sports day at school.
    Why does he feel sad about it?
    A He didn't win his race.
    B He lost his new sports shirt.
    C He couldn't do his favourite activity.

2   You will hear a girl talking to her friend about her new tennis racket.
    What does she say about it?
    A It belonged to a family member.
    B It was exactly what she wanted.
    C It was quite expensive.

3   You will hear a boy telling a friend about his winter sports holiday.
    Which activity did he like best?
    A skiing
    B snowboarding
    C walking in the mountains

4   You will hear a girl phoning her mum.
    Where is the girl now?
    A at the gym
    B at the pool
    C at the park

5   You will hear a boy phoning a friend about the hockey match they're playing in.
    Why does he think their team may win the match?
    A They have some brilliant players.
    B They won against the other team before.
    C They've done lots of practice.

Vocabulary

do, *play* and *go* with sports

1 Put the letters in the right order to make the name of a sport. Then circle *do*, *play* or *go*.

1 skallbbeta   *do* / *play* / *go*   basketball
2 blicmngi   *do* / *play* / *go*   ....
3 hekyoc   *do* / *play* / *go*   ....
4 doju   *do* / *play* / *go*   ....
5 flobtalo   *do* / *play* / *go*   ....
6 miscnytsga   *do* / *play* / *go*   ....
7 madnobtin   *do* / *play* / *go*   ....

2 Complete the sentences with the correct form of the verb, *do*, *play* or *go*.

1 Josh can't come to your house. He .....'s playing.... tennis this evening.
2 Maria .... karate at the sports centre every Monday after school.
3 My parents sometimes .... badminton together.
4 I......................... running with my cousin tonight.
5 My teacher often .... cycling at the weekends.
6 Would you like to .... gymnastics with me next week at the sports centre?

Nationalities

3 Complete the sentences with the nationalities.

1 Luisa is from Spain.   She's .....Spanish..... .
2 Adriano is from Portugal.   He's ....
3 Ravi is from India.   He's ....
4 Agneta is from Sweden.   She's ....
5 Yumi is from Japan.   She's ....
6 Nicos is from Greece.   He's ....
7 Olivia is from Australia.   She's ....
8 Josh is from the USA.   He's ....

Writing Part 6

Look carefully at the verbs in the text, e.g. *ask*, *say*, *tell*. These tell you what to include in your answer.

Exam advice

1 Complete the email with the missing words.

I've got tickets to see a hockey match
(1) .... Saturday 16th January.
(2) .... you and your sister like
(3) .... come with me? The match is
(4) .... the stadium in town. It starts
at 2.30 pm in the (5) ....
(6) .... me know!
(7) .... you soon.

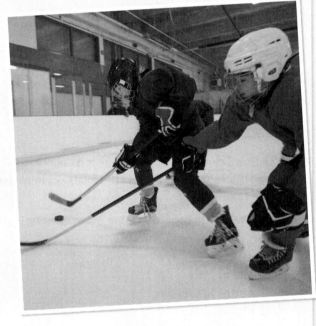

2 Now write an answer to this exam task.

You would like to go to the new sports centre in your town.

Write an email to your English friend, Olivia:

• invite Olivia to come with you
• tell Olivia when you can go
• say what you can do at the sports centre.

Write **25 words** or more.

5 Vocabulary extra

1a Match the sports with pictures 1–6.

1   2   3   4   5   6

climbing ..2..   cricket ....   running ....   sailing ....   skateboarding ....   tennis ....

1b Which sport from Exercise 1a is each sentence describing?

For this sport, you:

a hit the ball over the net with a racket.

........*tennis*........

b stand on a board with wheels on.

....

c need to go somewhere like a mountain.

....

d need a boat.

....

e can go on a road or round a sports field or track.

....

f hit the ball with a bat, and then run.

....

2 Find 11 more words connected to sport.

S	T	A	D	I	U	M	M
K	E	R	U	G	B	Y	A
A	N	A	G	O	L	F	T
T	N	C	B	A	T	M	C
I	I	E	G	L	B	N	H
N	S	K	I	I	N	G	P
G	R	A	C	K	E	T	O
S	U	R	F	I	N	G	M

3 Write the prices on the tags.

1 eighty-nine pence   **2** three hundred pounds

3 forty-five pounds fifty   **4** fifteen pounds ninety-seven pence

6 Have you got any homework?

Listening Part 3

1 For each question, choose the correct answer. You will hear Jamie and his sister Amelia talking about their first day back at school after the summer holiday.

1 What time did Amelia arrive at school?
- **A** 7.45
- **B** 8.15
- **C** 8.30

2 Which subject did Amelia have first?
- **A** physics
- **B** maths
- **C** biology

3 Jamie thinks his new timetable
- **A** has more difficult lessons than last year.
- **B** looks more interesting than last year.
- **C** is easier to remember than last year.

4 What did Amelia enjoy most about her day?
- **A** being in a different classroom
- **B** meeting new people
- **C** seeing her friends

5 What did Jamie forget to take with him?
- **A** his lunch
- **B** his football boots
- **C** his school bag

> Look carefully at each question to see what kind of information you're listening for.

Exam advice

Vocabulary

Classroom objects

1 Write the correct word for each sentence.

1 Your teacher might give you this to check you understand your lessons. t _e_ _s_ _t_

2 You can use this to help you draw a straight line. r _ _ _ _

3 You can write things in this that you want to remember. n _ _ _ _ _ _ _

4 You can check how to spell a word in this. d _ _ _ _ _ _ _ _ _

5 You can use this to draw pictures. p _ _ _ _ _

6 You look at this to find out which lessons you have each day. t _ _ _ _ _ _ _ _

7 You go here when you want to find a book to read. l _ _ _ _ _ _

8 You might wear this when you go to school. u _ _ _ _ _ _

Education verbs

2 Complete the sentences with the correct form of a verb from the box.

> fail   learn   pass   study   take   ~~teach~~

1 When I'm older, I'd like to ......_teach_...... English in a school.

2 If I don't do well in my exam, I can .... it again next month.

3 The best way to .... new words is to use them in sentences.

4 Sarah is always happy when she .... her exams!

5 My friend Sam wants to .... science at university.

6 I feel sad when I .... a test at school – but it doesn't happen very often!

Reading Part 2

Exam advice

Each answer will come from only one section of the text, so read the questions and sections carefully – there may be information in other sections that is similar to the answer.

I ♥ MATHS

Mandy

Maths is much easier for me now than other subjects like languages, but I found it hard when I started. My older sister isn't keen on maths, so my parents are pleased that I like it so much. Mr James is my maths teacher. We all talk about maths problems together in class and he explains things clearly – and he's really funny, too, so that's why we all like the subject.

Charlotte

I thought maths was quite easy when I had my first class and I loved trying to find the answers! I study at school with a really friendly group of girls in my class and we help each other and talk about our homework. Mrs Sams, my teacher, sometimes says we're too noisy, but she knows we're working hard! I love science, too, and I understand it much better now because my maths has improved.

Tina

My dad teaches maths at a college, so he's pleased I like it now. He says when I'm older I could study in his classes! So I'm thinking about that. Maths will help me to study science at a high level, too. But for now I'm just happy when I can do things like help my grandma count her money when we're shopping. My maths teacher is nice, but I don't know many people in my class. That means I work hard and don't chat!

---

1 For each question, choose the correct answer.

		Mandy	Charlotte	Tina
1	Who enjoys maths because of her teacher?	A	B	C
2	Who likes using maths outside school?	A	B	C
3	Who thinks learning maths has helped her with another school subject?	A	B	C
4	Who has someone in her family that doesn't like maths?	A	B	C
5	Who might study maths after she leaves school?	A	B	C
6	Who likes the other people in her maths class?	A	B	C
7	Who doesn't talk much in her maths class?	A	B	C

Grammar
have to

1 Read what Matt says about his hobby and complete the sentences with the correct form of the verb *have to*.

My name's Matt, and my favourite hobby is drawing. We usually (1) ....*have to*........ draw in art classes at school and I also go to an after-school drawing club with my friend Jake. We (2) .... take any paper or pencils because our teacher brings them, but she says we (3) .... go with some ideas about what to draw. Jake's great at art, and so he (4) .... ask the teacher for help. But sometimes my pictures aren't very good, so the teacher (5) .... give me some advice. She (6) .... tell us what to do very often though. At the end of each term, everyone (7) .... choose their best picture and put it on the school website for other students to look at. I hope they like mine this year!

6

2 Complete the questions using the correct form of *have to*. Then match them to the answers.

1 ....*Do*........ you ever ....*have to*.... tell your teacher that you haven't done your homework? [a]

2 .... you .... take a packed lunch to school? ☐

3 .... you .... get the bus to school? ☐

4 .... you .... wear a school uniform? ☐

5 .... your brother ever .... help you with your schoolwork? ☐

6 .... your parents sometimes .... collect you from school? ☐

a Yes, sometimes – when I've forgotten to do it!
b No, we can wear what we want at my school.
c Yes, with maths. He's much better at it than me.
d No, I can eat in the school café.
e Yes, if I'm sick and I need to go home.
f No, I usually ride my bike – it's not far.

Object pronouns

3 Look at the pictures from Jake's photo album. Complete what he says with the pronouns in the boxes.

> him ~~he~~ us

This is Mr Jones, our history teacher.(1) ......*He*...... teaches (2) .... three times a week, and everyone likes (3) ....

> it   they   we   us

I live with my family in this house. (4) .... all love (5) .... because there's a big garden. But my grandparents don't agree. (6) .... think the garden is too much work for my parents. So, Grandma sometimes comes to help (7) .... with our garden.

> I   it   them   they

These are my two older sisters.
(8) .... both live in America. (9) .... went to visit (10) .... last summer. (11) .... was a great trip.

Reading Part 5

First, read the whole text so you know what it is about. Then read each sentence carefully before you put a word in a gap.

Exam advice

1 For each question, write the correct answer. Write one word for each gap.

To: Anna
From: Sally

How's it going? (0) ......*Are*...... you excited about starting at our new school next week? I've just been into town with Mum to buy my uniform. I think it's much better (1) .... the one we had at our old school - especially the jumpers and T-shirts. (2) .... are both quite cool!

See what you think.

From: Sally
To: Anna

Yes, I agree (3) .... you about the new school uniform. (4) .... isn't as bad as our old one! Anyway, I still need to get (5) .... few things, so Mum says we have (6) .... go shopping in town tomorrow. I'll let you know when I've got everything!

6 Vocabulary extra

School and education

1 Look at the pictures. Put the letters in the right order to make the name of a school subject. Then match it with the examples of what you might study for that subject.

Subjects

1 scimu ...... *music*
2 lygoibo ....
3 sicshyp ....
4 pygagrohe ....
5 mythreics ....
6 soithyr..................
7 agluagnse ....
8 tasmh ....
9 trops ....

Examples

a what happened in the past
b how to play an instrument
c what salt is made of
d how to play football or tennis
e mountains and rivers
f German, Spanish and French
g animal and plant life
h electricity and space
i how to add numbers

2 Complete the sentences with the correct form of a verb in the box.

> collect   fail   leave   ~~repeat~~   study   teach   write

1 When I want to learn a new word, I ...*repeat*... it to myself lots of times.
2 When I .... school, I want to study at university.
3 It's important to do well in this exam, so I really don't want to ....
4 Peter never wants to .... at home by himself – he prefers playing football!
5 Mr Matthews .... us Maths and I understand everything in his classes.
6 Our teacher usually .... our homework on Tuesdays and gives it back to us on Fridays.
7 Janine often .... stories when she's at home – she has lots of great ideas.

3 Read the clues and complete the crossword.

Across
5 You look for new words in this.
6 You eat this meal in the middle of the day.
8 You have this short rest between lessons.
9 Your teacher will give you this to see how well you have understood your lessons.

Down
1 This tells you which classes you have each day.
2 This paper shows you have passed exams in a subject.
3 You might want to study here after you leave school.
4 You mustn't be this for your lessons!
7 This is a number of classes on one subject, often with an exam at the end.

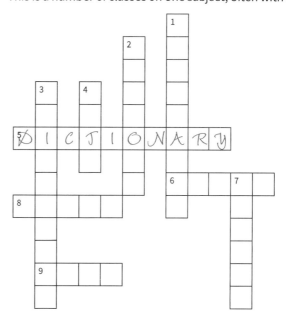

7 Let's go to the museum

Reading Part 1

> A text can be a notice, an email or a text message.

Exam advice

1 For each question, choose the correct answer.

1

**The door is for theatre staff only.
Please use the front entrance.**

A Nobody can use this door at the moment.
B You can only enter through here if you work at the theatre.
C The theatre is closed now.

2

Pattie,
I've got two cinema tickets for *Rainbows* tomorrow – come and join me! It starts at 2.30 pm. I can meet you there. Let me know!
Simon

A Simon wants to find out if Pattie has tickets for *Rainbows* tomorrow.
B Simon is asking Pattie to contact him about where to meet tomorrow.
C Simon is inviting Pattie to go with him to the film tomorrow.

3

TEENWEB.COM
Do you have a favourite film
that our readers will enjoy?
Write and tell us about it!
Click here for more information

A You can find out more information here about good films to enjoy.
B You can watch other people's favourite films on this website.
C You can send details of films that you think other people will like.

4

To: Students
From: Mr Morris

Can everyone who wants to go on the theatre trip please give me their ticket money by Wednesday, or we can't go.

A Mr Morris won't take students to the theatre if they don't pay on time.
B Mr Morris is checking which students want to join the theatre trip on Wednesday.
C Mr Morris says the theatre trip won't happen as not enough students are interested.

5

Maria,
Your kit for Saturday's Sports Day is in your cupboard. Let me know if anything needs washing. See you when I get home.
Dad

A Dad is letting Maria know where to find what she needs for Saturday.
B Dad is telling Maria her sports kit needs to go into the washing machine.
C Dad wants Maria to prepare her sports kit for Saturday before he comes home.

6

**THE MUSEUM IS CLOSED TODAY –
HEATING PROBLEMS**
**We are hoping to open tomorrow at 9 am
as usual, but please check our website
before you come.**

A Visitors need to look online to find the museum's usual opening times.
B You shouldn't go to the museum tomorrow until you've checked if it's open.
C Museum staff are sure they will repair the heating problems today.

Vocabulary
Buildings

1 Put the letters in the right order to make the names of places you can find in and around town.

1 usemum ....*museum*............
2 ratin tainsto ....
3 coftray ....
4 sholptia ....
5 itsdamu ....
6 hucrhc ....
7 ecanim ....
8 eomqsu ....

Directions

2 Fill in the missing words in the sentences. Use the words in the box.

bridge   crossing   ~~excuse~~   roundabout   square
straight   traffic   turning

1 ....*Excuse*............ me. Which way is the theatre?
2 Go .... on.
3 Take the first .... on the right.
4 To cross the river, go over the ....
5 Go right round the .... and take the last exit off it.
6 Go right at the .... lights.
7 It's safer to use the .... when you go across the road.
8 The town .... has shops on all four sides.

Listening Part 4

You will hear five different recordings, with questions for each one. Make sure you are ready to move on to the next question as each one starts.

Exam advice

---

1 08 For each question, choose the correct answer.

1 You will hear a boy telling a friend about a film he has just seen.
What did he enjoy most about it?
A the music
B the actors
C the story

2 You will hear a girl phoning her grandma to thank her for a present.
What was the present?
A something to wear
B something to read
C something to eat

3 You will hear a boy telling a friend about his visit to a gallery.
What did he enjoy about the visit?
A joining a class to do some painting
B copying another artist's painting
C seeing paintings he studied at school

4 You will hear Naomi talking about her train journey to her aunt's house.
What was the problem on her journey?
A The weather was bad.
B Her luggage was heavy.
C She had to stand.

5 You will hear a boy describing something in his garden.
What is he describing?
A the flowers
B the trees
C the birds

Grammar
Past simple

1 Complete the sentences using the correct form of the verbs in brackets.

1 My little brother ....*built*............ (build) a sandcastle on the beach yesterday.
2 I .... (throw) the ball to Karina, and she .... (catch) it.
3 I .... (sleep) late yesterday, so I .... (leave) the house later than usual.
4 My grandparents .... (drive) to our house to .... (give) me my birthday present.
5 I .... (hear) a noise outside my bedroom, and .... (see) my dog standing there.

7

2 👁 Exam candidates often make mistakes with the forms of irregular verbs.

Correct the mistakes in each of these sentences.

1 I didn't buy the jeans because they ~~costed~~ more than I expected. ......*cost*......

2 We really enjoied the party – we didn't want to go home! ....

3 Sam had a strawberry ice cream and I choosed a chocolate one. ....

4 My mum gived me some money to spend in town. ....

5 I buied a great magazine from my favourite shop yesterday. ....

6 Dan drinked so much lemonade that he couldn't eat his dinner. ....

3 Complete the sentences with the negative form of the underlined verbs.

1 At breakfast time, I <u>ate</u> some eggs and toast, but I ......*didn't eat*...... any fruit.

2 We <u>went</u> to Paris, but we .... into the centre. We visited my aunt outside the city.

3 Dad <u>bought</u> some tomatoes, but he .... any cheese.

4 When my brother left school, he <u>kept</u> his books, but he .... his uniform – he gave it to me.

5 Dad <u>drove</u> us home on the motorway, but he .... very fast.

6 It <u>was</u> sunny when we got up, but it .... sunny at the beach. It was raining!

4 Complete the questions to Ben about what he did yesterday using the verbs in brackets. Then match the questions to his answers.

1 What time did you get up ......*get up*...... (get up) yesterday morning? [c]

2 So where .... (be) in the morning? [ ]

3 And where .... (go) in the afternoon – into town? [ ]

4 How .... (get) there? In your dad's car? [ ]

5 .... (be) alone in the park? [ ]

6 .... (have) a good time? [ ]

a No, I went on the bus.
b No, I was with Josh and Amy.
c At 8.30.
d Yes, it was great, thanks!
e I was at home.
f No, I went to the park.

Imperatives

5 Imagine your friends are visiting your town. Tell them what to do and what not to do. Use these verbs.

buy ~~call~~ eat forget get travel

1 ......*Call*...... me when you arrive!
2 .... lost!
3 .... at the café in Main Street. The food's bad.
4 .... a map. It can help you to find your way.
5 .... your mobile phone. If you do, you won't be able to take any photos.
6 .... by bus everywhere. It's fun to walk!

Writing Part 6

Remember to start and finish your email correctly. **Exam advice**

1 Look at the different ways of starting and finishing an email to a friend. Tick (✓) the ones which should go at the <u>beginning</u> of an email.

Hi John, ✓
How are you? ....
Best wishes, ...
Dear Harry, ...
See you soon. ....
Thanks for your email. ....
It was nice to hear from you. ....
Bye for now. ....
Yours, ...

2 Read the email from your English friend, Rob.

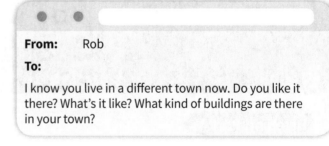

From: Rob
To:
I know you live in a different town now. Do you like it there? What's it like? What kind of buildings are there in your town?

3 Write an email to Rob. Write 25 words or more.

30

Town and city

 1 2  3  4 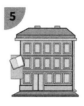 5  6  7 8

1a Match pictures 1–8 to the places.

castle *6*   garage .....   library .....   post office .....   police station .....   restaurant .....   supermarket .....   theatre .....

1b Match the names of places from Exercise 1a with their descriptions.

At this place, you can:

a borrow books.   .... *library* ....

b watch a play on stage.   ....

c buy some stamps and post a letter.   ....

d buy lots of food to cook at home.   ....

e ask about something you lost in the street.   ....

f see where people lived years ago.   ....

g have a meal.   ....

h ask someone to repair your car.   ....

2 Look at the map and complete the directions.

A: (1) ...... *Excuse* ...... me, how can I get to the supermarket (2) .... here?

B: Okay, go (3) .... on, then (4) .... left at the roundabout. Go (5) .... the bridge, and it's on your left.

A: Sorry, which way (6) .... the sports centre?

C: Go round the roundabout and take the (7) .... on the right. When you get to the library, go (8) .... the road. The sports centre is (9) .... the library.

A: (10) .... is the nearest café, please?

D: Go straight ahead, (11) .... the school. You'll find the café just by the traffic lights, (12) .... to the shopping centre.

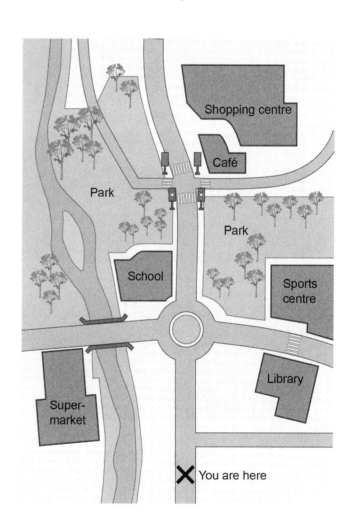

Shopping centre

Café

Park

Park

School

Sports centre

Library

Super-market

✗ You are here

8 Did you get my message?

Vocabulary
Technology verbs

1 Look at the pictures and write the activity. Use the expressions below. There is an extra expression you do not need to use.

> check your social media ~~download music~~
> email a friend   send a message   upload a selfie

1 ...... *download music* ......

2 ....

3 ....

4 ....

2 Answer these questions. Write complete sentences.

1 How many messages do you send your friends a day?
..... *I send fifty messages to my friends a day.* .....

2 Do you check your social media when you wake up?
....

3 Do you ever email your friends?
....

4 How often do you take selfies with your friends and upload them?
....

5 Do you download music or films from the internet?
....

Music

3a Order the letters to make kinds of music.

1 ajzz .... *jazz* ....
2 aeopr ....
3 opp ....
4 cceeilnotr ....
5 aaccillss ....
6 ckor ....
7 B&R ....

3b Write the kind of music next to these definitions. Use the words in Exercise 3a.

1 This type of music uses digital instruments and computers. .... *electronic* ....
2 Small bands of musicians often play this music, which comes from New Orleans, USA. ....
3 This type of music is often very loud. ....
4 Mozart, Bach and Beethoven wrote this kind of music. ....
5 Its full name is *popular music* because many people like it ....
6 *Rhythm and Blues* is its full name because it mixes blues with jazz. ....
7 Singers often sing this kind of music in a musical play. ....

Listening Part 5

Exam advice

You can only use each answer once. Remember to cross out the answers after you use them.

1 For each question, choose the correct answer. You will hear Max talking to a friend about what he and his friends did on Saturday. What activity did each person do?

09

People

0	Max	⌀
1	Josh	....
2	Matt	....
3	Elise	....
4	Susie	....
5	Nick	....

Activities

A   went out for food
B   played a computer game
C   played football
D   ~~read a book~~
E   saw a film
F   watched a match
G   went to a party
H   won a match

Grammar
Past continuous

1 Complete this conversation with the correct past continuous form of the verb in brackets.

Will: I tried to call you at 5 pm yesterday. What (1) ...*were you doing*... (you / do)?

Amy: I (2) .... (watch) a film on my computer. Why?

Will: We (3) .... (play) football in the park and we needed another player.

Amy: But it (4) .... (rain) at 5 pm! What (5) .... (your brother / do)?

Will: He (6) .... (upload) photos with his friends.

Amy: Really? I'll look at them on social media later.

2 Circle the correct words to complete the text.

Last Saturday I (1) *sit /* (*was sitting*) in the park with my friends when it (2) *started / was starting* to get cold so I (3) *decided / was deciding* to go home. While I (4) *downloaded / was downloading* a film, my cousin (5) *called / was calling* me. He (6) *wanted / was wanting* to go to the cinema. At 4 pm, I (7) *waited / was waiting* for him outside the cinema and I (8) *listened / was listening* to music on my phone. At that moment, I (9) *saw / was seeing* my favourite singer, so I (10) *took / was taking* a selfie with him!

3 Write complete sentences in the past simple and past continuous.

1   While / I / study / my brother / take / my phone.
    While I was studying, my brother took my phone.

2   Lily / wear / her new dress / when / I / meet / her.
    ....

3   We / watch / a film / when / we / hear / a strange noise.
    ....

4   When / you / call / me / I / have / dinner.
    ....

5   When / my dad / get home / my sister / listen to / music.
    ....

can / can't, could / couldn't

4 ◉ Exam candidates often make mistakes with *can / can't* and *could / couldn't*.

Correct the mistakes in each of these sentences.

1   My dad ~~can to take~~ great photos with his new phone.
    ...*can take*...

2   I can listening to music with this new app. ....

3   If you want, I could met you next Saturday.........................

4   We could to go there tomorrow.   ....

5   You can going by bus.........................

5 Complete these sentences with *can / can't* or *could / couldn't* and a verb from the box.

download   play   ride   speak   ~~swim~~

1   Mia learned to swim when she was five. She ...*could swim*... when she was six.

2   Jake's computer is broken so he .... any music at the moment.

3   Lucy is terrible at all sports. She .... basketball or volleyball.

4   Harvey is frightened of animals, so when he was on holiday, he .... a horse.

5   Sam .... three languages well: English, Italian and German.

Reading Part 2

Three young stars you should watch!

Aksel Rykkvin

Aksel is a classical singer from Norway. As a baby, his parents could see that he loved singing, so at five, he started singing in front of people and at eight, he started having singing lessons. Since then, Aksel has sung on TV and stage, on his own and in groups. When he was just 13, he became popular around the world. Millions have seen his YouTube videos and thousands like his Facebook page.

Oratilwe Hlongwane

Oratilwe was born in South Africa in 2012. At five he became the youngest person to put on the music in a club. It all began around his first birthday when Oratilwe's father gave him an iPad. He got bored of the games and began to use an app to make music instead. Oratilwe's videos on social media are very popular. For example, over 43 million have watched the one which shows him winning a TV talent show.

Shawn Mendes

Shawn is a Canadian pop singer. Until the age of 14, Shawn was a normal student who played football. His life changed when he uploaded a six and a half second music video to Vine. By the next morning, the video had 10,000 likes. A month later, Shawn played his first concert and just before he was 16, his first album got to number 1 on iTunes in 37 minutes. Millions of people now follow him on social media and thousands go to his concerts.

1 For each question, choose the correct answer.

		Askel	Oratilwe	Shawn
1	Which person was taught how to sing?	A	B	C
2	Which person began his career when he was the oldest?	A	B	C
3	Which person sometimes sings with other musicians?	A	B	C
4	Which person became famous when he became a teenager?	A	B	C
5	Which person used a present to make music?	A	B	C
6	Which person's album has been the most popular?	A	B	C
7	Which person came first in a TV competition?	A	B	C

Reading Part 5

1 Complete the email. Write one word for each gap.

From: Sebastian
To: Zoe

I had (0) ....A.... great time with my friends last weekend. On Saturday, we downloaded a film and then we watched it. While we (1) .... watching the film, my dad came home. He made some lemonade (2) .... us. After the film, we played computer games and listened to music.

On Sunday it was Toby's birthday party. He's (3) .... youngest in our class. I'm six months older (4) .... him. On his birthday, Toby got a (5) .... of presents. I bought him a book.

(6) .... you have a good weekend?

Love,

Sebastian

8 Vocabulary extra

Technology and music

1a Match 1–8 with a–h to make technology words.

1 soft
2 email
3 mobile
4 key
5 computer
6 digital
7 web
8 lap

a game
b camera
c ware
d top
e board
f site
g phone
h address

1b Complete the table with the words in Exercise 1a.

One word	Two words
software	email address

2 Complete these sentences with a verb. The first letter has been written for you. Then rewrite the sentences so they are true for you.

1 *I didn't call* my friends last weekend.
   I called some of my friends last weekend.

2 I often c _____ my phone for messages before I do my homework.

3 I usually s _____ messages to my friends 20 times a day.

4 I never d _____ my music from the internet.

5 When I am on holiday, I e _____ my friends every day.

6 I g _____ online at least twice a day.

3 Circle the correct word to complete these sentences.

1 I couldn't send you a message because I *failed / lost* my phone.

2 My brother *forgot / left* his phone on the bus yesterday.

3 Why don't we *do / go* shopping? There's a new clothes shop on Bridge Street.

4 My uncle *paid / spent* a lot of money on his new laptop.

5 I can't *listen / hear* the music. It's too quiet.

6 We *bought / paid* our teacher a jazz CD for his birthday.

4a Match the types of music 1–6 with the pictures A–F.

1 classical _C_
2 jazz _____
3 opera _____
4 pop _____
5 electronic _____
6 rock _____

4b Match the words a–f with 1–6 in the pictures in Exercise 4a.

a piano _3_
b guitar _____
c keyboard _____
d drum _____
e singer _____
f violin _____

9 I love that film!

Reading Part 4

Exam advice

Read the article carefully first. Think about the missing words before you start looking at the words A, B and C.

1 For each question, choose the correct answer.

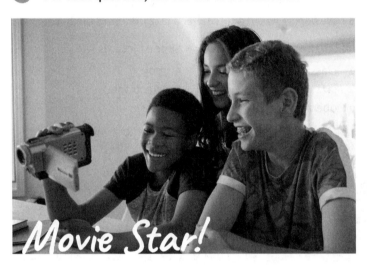

Movie Star!

Don't miss an amazing new film this year, Movie Star! In this awesome story, Stanley Marks is an out-of-work actor who dreams of becoming a movie star one day. However, he has lots of **(1)** .... luck. He loses his job as a waiter and needs to **(2)** .... some money. So he pretends to be an English teacher and starts working in a school. The students are interested in studying and getting good marks, but Stanley has another **(3)** .... He helps his students make a film, and they enter a national film competition. Will Stanley's students **(4)** .... ? What will the other teachers and parents say? If you want to know, you'll need to **(5)** .... a ticket and find out for yourself. You'll certainly **(6)** .... a lot of fun!

	A	**B**	**C**
1	wrong	bad	poor
2	take	earn	do
3	answer	reason	idea
4	pass	make	win
5	spend	buy	pay
6	have	like	get

Vocabulary

Suggesting, accepting and refusing

1 Read the dialogue. Write *S* (suggesting), *A* (accepting) or *R* (refusing) next to each line.

Tim: (1) Why don't we go to the cinema tonight? ...... S

Oscar: (2) I'd rather not. I haven't got any money. ....

Tim: (3) Would you like to watch a film at my house instead? ....

Oscar: (4) Sure. What film? ....

Tim: (5) How about a comedy? ....

Oscar: (6) Good idea. I'll bring some cola. ....

2 Complete the conversations with a suitable suggestion or reply. Use the expressions in the box.

> How about   OK
> I don't think so   thanks   Shall
> Would you like to

1 A: Why don't we go to the photography exhibition?
B: Umm,......*I don't think so*...... . I don't like exhibitions very much.

2 A: ....going shopping on Saturday?
B: Good idea. I need to buy some new shoes.

3 A: Why don't we play tennis?
B: Yes,.............................. Let's meet at the tennis club.

4 A: ....have pizza at my house this evening?
B: All right, that sounds good. I'll be there at 6 pm.

5 A: Let's go to the theatre.
B: No,.............................. . I think plays are boring.

6 A: ....we dance?
B: I'd rather not. I'm not very good at dancing.

Adjectives

3 Cross out the word which is <u>not</u> correct.

1 My favourite museum is the Science Museum.
It's *interesting* / ~~*terrible*~~ / *awesome*.

2 I didn't like the play. It was really *boring* / *terrible* / *amazing*.

3 I saw a great concert. It was *amazing* / *boring* / *awesome*.

4 There's a good film on TV. The actors are *amazing* / *awesome* / *horrible*.

5 I couldn't finish that book. It's *interesting* / *horrible* / *boring*.

6 We didn't enjoy the circus. We thought it was *awesome* / *terrible* / *horrible*.

Listening Part 2

Read the questions carefully before you listen and think about the missing information. You will need to write a word or a number.

Exam advice

1 For each question, write the correct answer in the gap. Write one word or a number or a date or a time. You will hear a woman talking on the radio about a magazine for young people.

New

ENTERTAINMENT MAGAZINE

Name: *What's On?*

Can buy every: **(1)** ....

Price: **(2)** £ ....

Wants articles about:
(3) ....

Prize for best article:
(4) ....

More information:
(5) ....@whatson.co.uk

Grammar
Verbs with *-ing* or *to* infinitive

1 Circle the correct words to complete the sentences.

1 We need (*to read*) / *reading* that play for our English class.

2 I wouldn't like *to be* / *being* famous.

3 My sister enjoys *to go* / *going* to the theatre.

4 It isn't easy *to work* / *working* as a dancer.

5 The group finished *to play* / *playing* at 9 pm.

6 My friends decided *to buy* / *buying* tickets for the film festival.

7 Thank you for *to download* / *downloading* the film. It's great!

8 My best friend wants *to dance* / *dancing* in the school show.

9 Don't worry about *to sing* / *singing* at my party. You sing really well!

2 Complete this email with the correct *-ing* or infinitive form of one of the verbs in the box.

be	dance	get	go
hear	see	~~send~~	sing

To: Luna

From: Clara

Hi Luna,

Thanks for **(1)** ....*sending*....... me a birthday present. My mum took me to see an amazing musical called *Matilda*. She says it wasn't easy
(2) .... the tickets because everyone wants **(3)** ....this show. The singing and dancing were awesome! I would love
(4) .... an actor in a musical but I'm not very good at
(5) .... or **(6)** ....
We're thinking of **(7)** .... to see the *Lion King* in May. Shall we get you a ticket?

I hope **(8)** .... from you soon.

Clara

3 Complete these sentences so they are true for you.

1 I'm tired of *playing computer games* .

2 I never promise ....

3 My best friend really enjoys
....

4 I don't mind ....

5 When I'm older, I don't want
....

6 It's difficult ....

> **The future with the present simple, present continuous and *will***

4 Circle the correct words to complete these sentences.

1 I'm sorry I can't go to the cinema later.
I'm having / 'll have dinner with my parents.

2 I'm bored. I know, I *call / 'll call* my friend to see if he wants to go swimming.

3 Remember the train *leaves / 'll leave* at 8 o'clock, so don't be late.

4 My best friend *comes / 's coming* to stay with me next week.

5 We're going to the circus. We think we're *having / 'll have* a great time.

6 The term *ends / 's ending* on Friday and then we're on holiday!

5 Write true answers to these questions. Use the present simple, present continuous or *will*.

1 What are you doing after school today?
I'm meeting my friends

2 What are your plans for Friday afternoon?
....

3 Would you like to go to an opera with me?
....

4 What time does school finish today?
....

5 Would you like pizza or pasta for dinner?
....

6 When is the next school holiday?
....

Writing Part 7

Look at the three pictures together and think of a possible story. Then write down some words which you can use in your story next to each picture.

Exam advice

1 Look at the three pictures. Write the words in the box under the correct picture.

> ~~feel bored~~   have fun   have a good idea
> make a poster   nothing to do   play the piano
> rain a lot   sing together   write invitations

.... *feel bored* ....
....
....

....
....
....

....
....
....

2 Look at the three pictures. Write the story shown in the pictures. Write <u>35 words</u> or more. (Try to use some of the words in Exercise 1).

9 Vocabulary extra

Entertainment and media

1 Match 1–10 with the words below.

actor ....4....   cinema ....   concert ....   photographer ....   picture ....

programme ....   screen ....   stage ....   theatre ....   ticket ....

2 Read the descriptions of some words about entertainment. What is the word for each one? The first letter is already there. There is one space for each other letter in the word.

1 A place where you can see films. c i n e m a
2 A person who moves his body to music. d _ _ _ _ _
3 People who play music together. g _ _ _ _
4 You can see this in a theatre. p _ _ _
5 A place where you can dance. d _ _ _ _
6 You can see photographs or pictures here. e _ _ _ _ _ _ _ _ _
7 A piano, a guitar and a violin are this. i _ _ _ _ _ _ _ _ _
8 Someone who plays an instrument. m _ _ _ _ _ _ _

3 Read these sentences. Are the adjectives good or bad? Write *G* (good) or *B* (bad).

1 I hated that film. It was <u>terrible</u>.   B
2 My brother's pop group are <u>excellent</u>! I love them. ⬜
3 I didn't enjoy the photography exhibition. It was <u>awful</u>. ⬜
4 My sister's interested in theatre. She says it's <u>cool</u>. ⬜
5 I saw a great show last week.It was <u>brilliant</u>. ⬜
6 The story was very nice. It was <u>pleasant</u>. ⬜

10 It's going to be sunny

Remember to listen to all the conversation before you choose the answer.

Exam advice

1 For each question, choose the correct answer.

1 What is Sophie doing now?

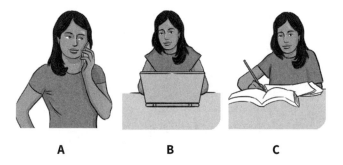

A   B   C

2 What will the weather be like tomorrow?

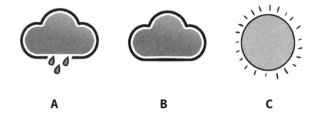

A   B   C

3 What time does Harriet's party start?

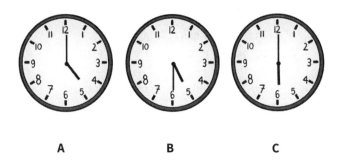

A   B   C

4 How many people are in Matt's band?

A   B   C

5 What was Owen wearing yesterday?

A   B   C

Vocabulary
What's the weather like?

1 Complete these sentences with the words in the box.

cold   foggy   ~~hot~~   snowing   raining   windy

1 Why don't you take off your jumper? It's 26°C. Aren't you ....._hot_..... ?
2 The trees are moving a lot because it's ....
3 Everything's white outside. Is it .... ?
4 We can't play football today because we can't see the ball. It's really ....
5 I'm going to put on my warm coat, because it's .... outside this morning.
6 It's .... and I don't have an umbrella, so I need to stay in the classroom to eat my lunch.

Places

2 Order the letters to make places.

1 akle   *lake*
2 rfoste   ....
3 inotmuna   ....
4 adnsil   ....
5 chbae   ....
6 seetdr   ....

Reading Part 2

Exam advice

Do <u>not</u> choose an answer just because the same words appear in the question and the text.

1 For each question, choose the correct answer.

		Marie	Candy	Ambar
1	Which person is going to visit members of her family?	A	B	C
2	Which person's family wants to feel warmer this winter?	A	B	C
3	Which person will ride an animal?	A	B	C
4	Which person won't be able to visit an island on holiday?	A	B	C
5	Which person is worried about the journey?	A	B	C
6	Which person is going to be away for more than two weeks?	A	B	C
7	Which person should take warm clothes?	A	B	C

Grammar

going to

1 Write sentences with (*not*) *going to.*

1 We're late. (miss the bus)
   We're going to miss the bus.
2 I hate parties. (not have a good time)
   ....
3 I haven't got a coat. (be cold)
   ....
4 The sky is blue. (not rain)
   ....
5 We studied a lot for the exam. (not fail)
   ....
6 Your little sister looks sad. (cry)
   ....

Young travel bloggers write about their next holiday

Marie

Last week, I wrote about my winter holiday in Iceland with my family, so I guess I should tell you about my next trip. Our football team is going to Morocco in April for 10 days – I can't wait! We're going to start in the capital Rabat, where we'll play a few matches. Then we'll have a day trip in the desert on a camel and two days climbing in the mountains. Our coach says we'll need to pack for hot and cold weather.

Candy

We're going to Costa Rica in just over two weeks! Yesterday Dad booked us a seven-day trip because we were all very cold this January. Everyone says it's a beautiful green country with rainforests, national parks and mountains. Mum loves nature, so I'm sure she'll take lots of photos. I'm a bit afraid of wild animals like monkeys, but I'm excited about the journey. Unfortunately, we won't have time for Tortuga Island, which has cool beaches.

Ambar

I can't believe it! I'm going to Japan next July for almost three weeks. My cousins live in the capital, so they're going to pick me up at the airport. Don't tell anyone but I'm scared of flying – I hope it isn't windy. Tokyo is very warm in July, so we'll probably go to Hokkaido, an island in the north. We'll visit the city of Sapporo for the jazz festival and then camp in the forest, so we can ride our bikes.

2 Write questions with *going to* and the verb in brackets. Then write true answers for you.

1 Who *are you going to send a message* (send/message) to after school?
I'm going to send a message to my best friend.

2 Where .... (your family / have) dinner tonight?
....

3 What time .... (you / wake up) tomorrow?
....

4 What .... (the weather / be like) tomorrow?
....

5 When .... (your teacher / give) your class a test?
....

6 Who .... (you / see) at the weekend?
....

must / mustn't

3 ◉ Exam candidates often make mistakes with *must* and *mustn't*. Correct the mistakes in each of these sentences.

1 You must ~~to wear~~ old clothes.
.............*wear*.............

2 I must to learn a very long and difficult lesson.
....

3 I must going to school by car.
....

4 You must visiting your grandfather.
....

5 We musn't use our phones in class.
....

6 We have lots of things to eat. You mustn't bring any food.
....

4 Look at the rules. Then complete these sentences with *must* or *mustn't* and a suitable verb.

HILLSIDE PARK RULES
✓ Leave your bicycle outside the park
✓ Take your empty bottles home
✓ Walk on the paths
✓ Use the bridge
✗ Play ball sports anywhere
✗ Swim in the lake
✗ Climb trees
✗ Light a fire

1 You ....*must walk*.......... on the paths.
2 You .... trees in the forest.
3 You .... ball sports anywhere.
4 You .... your empty bottles home.
5 You .... a fire.
6 You .... in the lake.
7 You .... the bridge to cross the river.
8 You .... your bicycle outside the park.

Reading Part 5

> If you need to write a verb in the space, check that you use the right form or tense.
>
> **Exam advice**

1 For each question, write the correct answer. Write one word in each gap.

To: Abigail

From: Isobel

Hi Abigail,

We're going to Rainbow Forest **(0)** ....*on*.......... Saturday. Would you like to come? My uncle **(1)** .... going to drive, so why don't we pick you up at 9 am? The forest is beautiful **(2)** .... the autumn. My aunt wants to walk to the lake and we're going to rent **(3)** .... boat there. I think it's a great idea. We can have lunch on the island.

You **(4)** .... probably bring warm clothes and walking boots because it's often cold there. Don't worry **(5)** .... bringing food or money.

Call me if **(6)** .... can come.

Isobel

10 Vocabulary extra

The natural world

1a Write the name of the season under the pictures A–D.

A _summer_   **B** ....   **C** ....   **D** ....

1b Read the weather descriptions 1–4 below and match them with the pictures in Exercise 1a.

1 It's quite warm this morning. It's not raining but it's a little bit foggy.   _D_

2 There's ice on the road and it's snowing.   ....

3 It isn't very cold but it's wet and windy because there's a storm.   ....

4 It's very hot. There aren't any clouds and the sun is high in the sky.   ....

2a Label the picture with the words in the box.

> beach   desert   forest   island   lake
> mountain   path   river   sea   ~~sky~~

1 _sky_   **2** ....   **3** ....   **4** ....   **5** ....
6 ....   **7** ....   **8** ....   **9** ....   **10** ....

2b Complete the email with some of the words in Exercise 2a.

To: Adam

From: Bruno

Hi Adam,

We're having a great time in Italy. The countryside is amazing. Yesterday morning we went up Mont Blanc, which at 4810m is the highest **(1)** _mountain_ in Europe. The weather was awesome. There wasn't a cloud in the **(2)** ...., so the views were brilliant. In the afternoon we walked along a **(3)** ....
through a beautiful **(4)** ....
The trees were amazing. Today we're going to take a boat across **(5)** .... Maggiore to a small **(6)** .... in the middle. Tomorrow it's going to be very hot, so we're going to drive to the sea. I want to lie down on the **(7)** ....
and rest.

Are you having a good holiday?

Write soon,

Bruno

Reading Part 3

1 For each question, choose the correct answer.

Meet Charlotte Simmonds, a young surf life-saver.

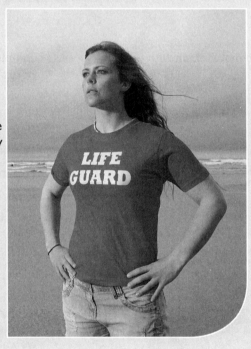

Charlotte Simmonds is a 17-year-old student from Sydney, Australia. Charlotte spends a lot of her spare time on the beach because she is also a surf life-saver. Her job is to save the lives of people on the beach or in the water, but she doesn't get any money for this. She does it because she wants to help.

When she's older, she hopes to work as a life-saver in some of the most famous surf beaches in the world, like Arugam Bay in Sri Lanka or Pipeline in Hawaii. However, first she wants to go to James Cook University in Australia to study Marine Biology.

Charlotte joined the Nippers Surf Life-Saving Club with her older brother when she was just five years old. 'We lived near the beach but my parents were very busy in their shop. This club was a great way to meet other children, stay fit and healthy and most importantly, we could spend hours on the beach. Like most of my friends, we learned to swim and surf when we were young. At the age of 15 I became a surf life-saver and soon after that I saved somebody in the sea. This year, Australian life-savers have already helped nearly 11,000 people.'

Charlotte loves looking after people on the beach. 'Everyone can see us on the beach because we wear red and yellow hats, shirts and shorts. If you can't see us that means we can't see you, so maybe you aren't safe.'

> **Exam advice**
>
> Read the article first. Then read the questions carefully and underline the important words in each one. Finally, underline the answers in the article.

1 What does Charlotte say about her job?
  A She earns a lot.
  B She isn't paid much money.
  C She doesn't want to be paid.

2 In the future, Charlotte would like to
  A study in a foreign country.
  B become a famous surfer.
  C do a similar job somewhere else.

3 What does Charlotte say about her family?
  A They had a lot of free time together.
  B They had a small business.
  C They lived far from the beach.

4 When did Charlotte first help a swimmer?
  A When she was very young.
  B When she was 15.
  C When she was 17.

5 What advice does Charlotte give to people on the beach?
  A Make sure you can see the life-saver!
  B Look after other people on the beach!
  C Don't forget to wear a hat!

Vocabulary
Parts of the body

1 Find 11 more parts of the body.

H	B	A	C	K	H	R	M	O	G
Y	C	B	M	J	V	E	C	S	K
F	Q	A	V	F	Z	G	S	C	I
Z	O	D	M	H	L	N	G	O	G
I	L	O	T	O	Q	I	H	M	N
K	G	U	T	P	T	F	A	R	U
J	O	K	C	E	N	S	N	A	E
M	I	Y	E	E	H	F	D	Y	L
Z	H	E	A	D	J	E	E	L	E
C	M	U	M	Y	K	B	W	N	G

What's the matter?

2a Match the verbs 1–6 with a–f to make expressions.

1 feel   a to the dentist
2 take   b some water
3 go   c sick
4 have (got)   d down in bed
5 drink   e an aspirin
6 lie   f a temperature

2b Complete these sentences with the expressions in Exercise 2a.

1 When I've got a headache, I take an ....*aspirin*............ .
2 If you eat a lot of cakes, you will ....
3 You won't be thirsty if you ....
4 When I've got a toothache, I usually
   ....
5 You look tired. Why don't you .... ?
6 I've got a bad cold and I ....
   I'm so hot!

Listening Part 4

Remember you won't always hear the same words as in the question. Listen and try to understand the main idea.

Exam advice

1 For each question, choose the correct answer.

12

1 You will hear a boy talking to his teacher.
   Why didn't he go to school in the morning?
   A His hand hurt.
   B He had a toothache.
   C He felt ill.

2 You will hear a tennis coach talking to a player.
   What's the weather like today?
   A It's wet.
   B It's cloudy.
   C It's sunny.

3 You will hear two friends talking about next weekend.
   What are they going to do?
   A They're going to a concert.
   B They're going shopping.
   C They're going to a friend's party.

4 You will hear a teacher talking to her class.
   Where are they going on the school trip?
   A a pool
   B a river
   C a lake

5 You will hear two friends talking about a show.
   What do they say about it?
   A Some parts were funny.
   B The music was awesome.
   C They didn't see the whole show.

Grammar
First conditional

1 Circle the correct answer.

1 If we play tennis inside the classroom, our teacher (will) / won't get angry.
2 If it's warm, I 'll wear / won't wear my coat.
3 If it rains / doesn't rain, we'll go cycling.
4 You won't understand if you listen / don't listen.
5 If you are / aren't hungry, my dad will make some sandwiches.
6 If he studies hard, he 'll pass / won't pass the test.

2 Use the correct form of the verb in brackets to complete the conversation.

Ruby: What are you doing tomorrow?
Josh: I'm going to Blakemore Forest with my cousins.
Ruby: What (1) will you do (you / do) if the weather (2) .... (be) bad?

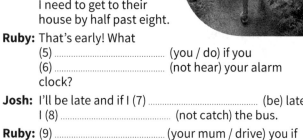

Josh: If it (3) .... (rain), we (4) .... (visit) the Science Museum instead. The only problem is that I need to get to their house by half past eight.
Ruby: That's early! What (5) .... (you / do) if you (6) .... (not hear) your alarm clock?
Josh: I'll be late and if I (7) .... (be) late, I (8) .... (not catch) the bus.
Ruby: (9) .... (your mum / drive) you if you (10) .... (miss) the bus?
Josh: No, she can't. She leaves for work at 7.30am.

3 Write true answers to these questions.

1 What will you do if you wake up late tomorrow?
If I wake up late, I'll miss the school bus.
2 What will you buy if you go shopping this afternoon?
....
3 Will your friends worry if you don't go to school tomorrow?
....
4 Where will you go if it's sunny on Saturday?
....
5 What will you do if you meet your friends at the weekend?
....

something, anything, nothing, etc.

4 Choose the correct words in the letter.

Hi Oliver,
We've got a new sports teacher and (1) anyone / everyone likes him. Yesterday we did (2) anything / something different. The teacher gave (3) everything / everyone a large ball and we had to do some exercises. (4) Nothing / Nobody was bored in that class. I've got (5) anything / something else to tell you. We've got (6) someone / everyone new in our class – your cousin! Have you done (7) everything / anything interesting this week?
Jimmy

5 Answer these questions with some-, any-, no-, every- pronouns.

1 Has anyone in your family got blue eyes?
No, no one in my family has got blue eyes.
2 Have you got anything to eat in your school bag?
....
3 Does anyone in your family go running?
....
4 Can everyone in your class speak English?
....
5 Did you do anything interesting last night?
....

Writing Part 6

Make sure you answer all three questions. Then check your work for spelling, punctuation and grammar.

Exam advice

1 Read the email from your English friend, Alex. Underline the three questions you need to answer.

From: Alex
To:
I'm glad that you can come skating on Saturday. What time would you like to meet? Where shall we go to skate? Where do you want to have lunch afterwards?

2 Write an email to Alex and answer the questions. Write 25 words or more.

11 Vocabulary extra

Health, medicine and exercise

1 Match 1–10 with the words below.

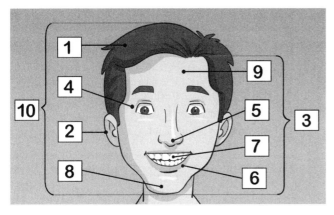

chin ..8..   forehead ......   nose ......
ear ......   hair ......   tooth ......
eye ......   head ......
face ......   mouth ......

2 Label the parts of the skater a–l. The first letter is already there.

a n......eck......   e f......   i l......
b s......   f t......   j k......
c a......   g b......   k a......
d h......   h s......   l f......

3a What health problem have they got? Read the description and write a sentence.

1 I don't feel well. My nose hurts.
  .You've got a cold.

2 Nicola's tooth hurts.
  ....

3 I feel very hot.
  ....

4 My leg hurts and I can't move it.
  ....

5 Jack's head hurts.
  ....

6 We ate something bad and our stomachs hurt.
  ....

3b Complete the health advice. The first letter is already there. Then match a–f with 1–6 in Exercise 3a.

a Theres ......nothing...... you can do, except rest.   ☑ 1
b Don't g .... to school.
   L .... d .... in bed.   ☐
c D .... some water.   ☐
d C .... an ambulance and
   g .... to hospital.   ☐
e T .... an aspirin.   ☐
f G ....to the dentist.   ☐

4 Write the ordinal number.

1st	....first....	**15th**	....
2nd	....	**19th**	....
3rd	....	**20th**	....
4th	....	**21st**	....
5TH	....	**30TH**	....
9th	....	**31st**	....

12 Have you ever been on a plane?

Reading Part 1

> **Exam advice**
> Don't match a notice with an answer just because the words are the same.

1 For each question, choose the correct answer.

1

Win free burgers for a year!
Upload a photo with your friends at Bings!

A The food at Bings is free.
B Bings is having a competition.
C You will like the burgers at Bings.

2

Be careful. Busy road!
Get off your bike and use the crossing!

A You can't ride on the bike path.
B You mustn't get off your bike to cross the road.
C You shouldn't ride your bike across the street.

3

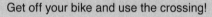

Hi Oscar,
Mum has booked our cinema tickets online. Can you bring the money to school before Friday?
Thanks,
Jade!

A Jade wants Oscar to buy the cinema tickets.
B Jade's mum has found a good website.
C Oscar should pay for his cinema ticket soon.

4

Daily concerts here!
Adults €15. Under-18s half price today only.
Cash only.

A You can't pay by credit card.
B It's cheaper for over 18s.
C The concert is only on today.

5

Your download is ready ✕
Click to start.
Download three more songs for free!

A You must do something if you want to download a song.
B You can listen to your favourite songs online for free.
C If you want to listen to three songs, you'll have to pay.

6
Mark,
I'm on the platform. The train leaves in 5 minutes. If you're going to be late, text us and we'll catch the next one.
Paula

What should Mark do?
A meet Paula inside the station
B tell Paula if she should catch a different train
C catch the next train

Vocabulary
Means of transport

1 Look at the vehicles and complete the crossword.
What's the secret word?

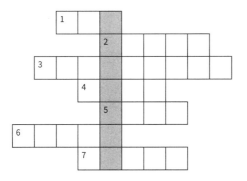

Secret word: _ _ _ _ _ _ _

Travel verbs

2 Complete the sentences with *drive, fly* or *ride*.

1 I often ...._ride_........ my bike to school. It's the quickest way to get there.

2 My dad started to .... a taxi when he was 20.

3 My cousin's hurt his leg, so he can't .... his motorbike.

4 You can .... in a helicopter over many capital cities to see amazing views.

5 It's easier to .... a tram than a train, but both jobs are difficult.

6 We're going to .... to Hong Kong in an Airbus A380. They're enormous planes.

Listening Part 2

Check your spelling carefully, especially if the spelling is given on the recording. **Exam advice**

1 For each question, write the correct answer in the gap. Write one word or a number or a date or a time. You will hear a teacher telling his students about their trip to Lisbon.

School trip to Lisbon	
Cost of trip:	....._£225_.....
Pay money by:	(1) .... April
Be at school at:	(2) .... am
On first day in Lisbon, travel by:	(3) ....
Bring:	(4) ....
For more details, contact:	(5) .... Nºschool.com

Grammar
Present perfect

1a Complete the table.

	infinitive	past simple	past participle
1	drive	_drove_	driven
2	....	drank	drunk
3	eat	ate	....
4	swim	swam	....
5	....	visited	visited
6	write	wrote	....

1b Complete these sentences in the present perfect affirmative or negative. Use the verbs in Exercise 1a.

1 My sister _hasn't eaten_ her lunch because she's sick.

2 I haven't got my grandmother's address, so I .... a letter to her.

3 My cousin .... with dolphins in the Pacific Ocean. Can you believe it?

4 You're thirsty because you .... any water.

5 My uncle loves vehicles. He .... a taxi, a bus and a coach.

6 My aunt is from Paris but she .... the Eiffel Tower.

12

2 👁 Exam candidates often make mistakes with infinitive, past simple and past participle forms. Correct the mistakes in each of these sentences.

1 I have ~~writed~~ a letter to him. ....*written*..........
2 My father's going to drove there. ....
3 We've ate in a famous restaurant. ....
4 I went to the beach and I swum every day. ....
5 I bouth new jeans last week. ....
6 He's drank a lot of lemonade. ....

3 Use the verb in brackets to complete these questions. Then write the short answer.

1 ......*Has*...... your father ever ......*lived*...... (live) in Africa? No, ...*he hasn't*.......
2 .... you ever .... (read) a play by Shakespeare? No, ...
3 .... your older brother ever .... (drive) a car? Yes, ...
4 ....your friends ever .... (travel) by plane? Yes, ...
5 .... you ever ....(miss) a class at school? Yes, ...
6 .... we ever .... (be) in a helicopter? No, ...

should / shouldn't

4 Circle the correct words to complete the advice.

HOW TO BE COMFORTABLE ON A LONG JOURNEY!

Follow this advice!

- **TRY TO GET SOME SLEEP!**
- You (1) *should /(shouldn't)*wear uncomfortable clothes or shoes.
- You (2) *should / shouldn't* bring a small travel pillow.
- **DON'T GET HUNGRY OR THIRSTY!**
- You (3) *should / shouldn't* take lots of your favourite foods, snacks and drinks.
- You (4) *should / shouldn't* eat food with a lot of salt. You'll get thirsty!
- **DON'T GET BORED!**
- You (5) *should / shouldn't* download a film, music or a game before the journey.
- You (6) *should / shouldn't* try to play any difficult games where you have to think a lot.

5 Complete the sentences with *should / shouldn't* and the verb in brackets.

1 Dad's sleeping. You and your friends ....*should be*......... (be) quieter.
2 It's hot in here. He .... (take off) his jumper.
3 It's very windy. We .... (go) on a boat.
4 I felt sick yesterday. I .... (eat) very much today.
5 We saw an awesome film. You .... (see) it!
6 We've got a lot of exams next week. We .... (have) a party this weekend.

Writing Part 7

Make sure you check your spelling carefully.

Exam advice

1 👁 Exam candidates often make mistakes with spelling. Correct five spelling mistakes in this story. The first one has been done as an example.

Last Saturday I went with my family to ~~by~~ *buy* some new clothes. We looked at many intresting things. In the sports shop, I saw some beatiful blue trainers but they were to expensive. In the end I bought some red ones becouse they were much cheaper.

2 Look at the three pictures. Write the story shown in the pictures. Write 35 words or more.

12 Vocabulary extra

Travel and transport

1 Look at the picture and write the vehicles. The first letter is already there.

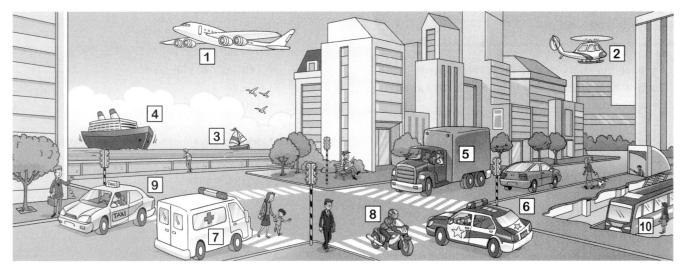

1 p l a n e
2 h _ _ _ _ _ _ _ _ _
3 b _ _ _
4 s _ _ _
5 l _ _ _ _

6 p _ _ _ _ _ c _ _
7 a _ _ _ _ _ _ _ _
8 m _ _ _ _ _ _ _ _
9 t _ _ _
10 u _ _ _ _ _ _ _ _ _

2a Match the travel verbs 1–10 with the descriptions a–j.

1 drive
2 get on
3 fly
4 ride
5 park
6 miss
7 return
8 get off
9 sail
10 catch

a come back to a place
b travel by bike
c make a car move from one place to another
d put a car in a place for a while
e travel by boat or ship
f take a bus, plane, train etc.
g travel by plane
h be too late to catch a bus
i leave a bus, plane, train etc.
j enter a bus, plane, train etc.

2b Complete these sentences with some of the verbs in Exercise 2a.

1 How often do you ....ride........ your bike to school?
2 If you wake up late, you'll .... the bus.
3 My mum loves driving but she can't .... the car in the city centre.
4 This summer we're going to .... around the Greek islands in a boat.
5 If we want to .... the early coach, we'll have to leave home at 6.30 am.

3 Complete the table.

	infinitive	past simple	past participle
1	catch	caught	caught
2	come		
3	find		
4	fly		
5	get		
6	hear		
7	leave		
8	meet		
9	ride		

13 What's your hobby?

Listening Part 3

Exam advice

Don't worry if you don't hear the answer the first time you listen. You will listen to the conversation twice.

1 For each question, choose the correct answer. You will hear Josh talking to his friend Kyra about snowboarding.

1 What is Josh going to buy?
   A new clothes for school
   B something to wear to do sport
   C a new snowboard

2 When is Josh going snowboarding?
   A Thursday
   B Friday
   C Saturday

3 How much did Josh's snowboard cost?
   A £40
   B £80
   C £90

4 Josh starts snowboarding at
   A 8.00 am.
   B 9.00 am.
   C 10.00 am.

5 Kyra thinks snowboarding is
   A dangerous.
   B amazing.
   C terrible.

Vocabulary
Adverbs

1 Rewrite these sentences with an adverb. Use the word in CAPITAL LETTERS.

1 We did our Maths homework.   BAD
   We did our Maths homework badly.

2 My brother can play chess.   GOOD
   ....

3 My little sister runs.   QUICK
   ....

4 My friends are going to win the competition.   EASY
   ....

5 I'll carry the cake.   CAREFUL
   ....

6 We played cards.   HAPPY
   ....

Jobs

2 Read the sentence and write the job. Use the words in the box.

> coach   journalist   mechanic   nurse
> photographer   ~~pilot~~   vet

1 Right now we're flying at 9,000 metres above the ground. ....*pilot*..........

2 Can I ask you some questions for the newspaper, please?..............................

3 That's a good position. Don't move! And smile!
   ....

4 How long has your dog been ill?..............................

5 I'm going to clean the cut on your hand. Don't worry! It won't hurt...........................

6 I'd like you all to run around the stadium three times. Go!..........................

7 Shall I check your tyres?..............................

Reading Part 3

1 For each question, choose the correct answer.

Marina Martin, a young games tester

Most days I finish my homework and then I have to play computer games for the rest of the afternoon. Yes, I have to! You see, I earn money by looking for mistakes in games.

I've always been crazy about computer games. My dad's a journalist and my mum's a photographer, so there's been a computer in the house since before I was born. I can remember playing very simple games on it when I was less than five years old and my dad telling me to switch it off and go outside.

I was online one day when I saw an advertisement from a video game company. They were looking for young people to give their opinions about some of their new games. I contacted them but I wasn't old enough because I was 14.

Three years later, several companies now send me their games. I often spend hours on the same game. I have to play it from start to finish several times, look at all the menus and try all the different ways of playing it. While I'm doing this, I take notes and then write a clear email which the company can understand easily.

You have to work quickly because the company often wants to sell their new game as soon as possible. I may have to spend a lot of the weekend testing. However, I think I'm very lucky that my hobby has become a job. Most of the time, I love it!

1 What does Marina say about computer games?
 A She plays them to take a break from studying.
 B Somebody pays her to play them.
 C Lots of them have got mistakes in them.

2 Marina has been interested in computer games since
 A her mum became a photographer.
 B her dad bought her a computer.
 C she was a small child.

3 What happened when Marina was 14 years old?
 A She didn't get a job as a games tester.
 B She found an advertisement for a new video game.
 C She started to use the internet.

4 What does Marina do as part of her job?
 A She teaches other people how to play the game.
 B She makes sure that she wins all the games.
 C She checks each game carefully more than once.

5 How does Marina feel about her job?
 A She almost always enjoys it.
 B She doesn't want to do anything else.
 C She thinks it can be boring.

Grammar

Present perfect with *for* and *since*

1 Complete the table with the time expressions.

last week   a long time   months   my sister's birthday   September   ~~three years~~   ~~1998~~

for	since
three years	1998

2 Write complete sentences with the present perfect and *for* or *since*.

1 My mum / work in the post office / 16 years.
My mum's worked in the post office for 16 years

2 Our teacher / be ill / three days.

3 I / not dance / your birthday party.

4 My uncle and aunt / have their car / three months.

5 My best friend / not call me / last week.

3 Write complete questions with *How long ...?* Then write answers that are true for you with *for* or *since*.

1 you like your favourite sport?

How long have you liked your favourite sport?
I've liked football for a long time.

2 your teacher work at your school?

....

....

3 you have your pencil case?

....

....

4 you live in your house?

....

....

5 your best friend be at your school?

....

....

....

> **may / might**

4 Complete the conversation with the phrases in the box. There are two phrases you do not need.

> may enjoy   may not do   may not like
> may see   ~~may stay~~   might call   might go
> might have   might not be

Harry: What are you doing this afternoon?

Alice: I (1) *may stay* at home or I (2) .... to my grandmother's house. What about you?

Harry: My cousin Jack (3) .... me. If he does, we (4) .... a film at the cinema. Would you like to come?

Alice: Perhaps but I (5) .... here. What's on?

Harry: There's a new adventure film about the Sahara Desert but you (6) .... it.

Alice: Probably not, I don't like adventure films very much. What are you going to do afterwards?

Harry: We (7) .... pizza. I'll send you a message.

Alice: Thanks, Harry.

5 Rewrite the sentences with the word in brackets.

1 It's possible we will win the match. (may)

We may win the match.

We may win the match.

2 My sister could be late. (might)

....

3 It's possible my friends won't snowboard at the weekend. (might not)

....

4 You could have a broken hand. (may)

....

5 We may buy a new laptop. (might)

....

> **Writing Part 6**

Remember to begin and end an email correctly and to answer all three points in the question.

Exam advice

1 Read the Writing Part 6 question below carefully and underline the three points you need to write about.

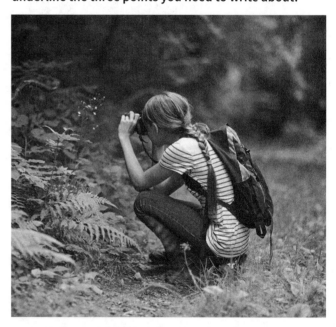

You'd like to do a photography course. Write an email to your English friend, Gabby.

- **Invite** Gabby to do the course with you.
- **Tell** Gabby why you want to do the course.
- **Say when** the course begins.

2 Now write an email to Gabby. Write 25 words or more.

13 Vocabulary extra

Work and leisure

1a Match the people 1–12 in the picture with the jobs below.

artist	*12*	photographer	....
coach	....	pilot	....
dentist	....	receptionist	....
journalist	....	shop assistant	....
mechanic	....	vet	....
nurse	....	waiter	....

1b Find five hobbies a–e in the picture.

doing puzzles	*d*	skateboarding	....
listening to music	....	taking photographs	....
painting	....		

2 Match the jobs 1–8 with the places of work a–h.

1 police officer   a department store
2 doctor   b farm
3 mechanic   c pharmacy
4 businessperson   d restaurant
5 chef   e hospital
6 farmer   f office
7 shop assistant   g police station
8 chemist   h garage

3a Complete the table with the adverbs.

	Adjective	Adverb
1	slow	*slowly*
2	terrible	
3	good	
4	safe	
5	quiet	
6	fast	
7	noisy	

3b Look at the adverb in A's question. Then complete B's answer with a different adverb with an <u>opposite</u> meaning. Use some of the adverbs in Exercise 3a.

1 A Does she eat quickly?
  B No, she eats ...... *slowly* ....

2 A Do you draw badly?
  B No, I don't. I can draw really ....

3 A Does your new teacher speak slowly?
  B No, she speaks very ....

4 A Did your team play brilliantly?
  B No, we didn't. We played ....

5 A Were you riding your bike dangerously?
  B No, I was riding it ....

14 Keep in touch!

Listening Part 5

> **Exam advice**
>
> Listen carefully to the whole conversation. Don't choose an answer just because it is the first word you hear on the list.

1 For each question, choose the correct answer. You will hear Annabelle talking to a friend about her family. How does each family member contact her?

People

0	uncle	..G..
1	aunt	....
2	cousin	....
3	brother	....
4	grandma	....
5	mum	....

Communication

A blog

B card

C call

D email

E letter

F note

G postcard

H text message

Vocabulary
Communication verbs

1a Read the description of some communication verbs. What is the word for each one? The first letter is already there. There is one space for each letter in the word.

1 This is when you say something again. r _e_ _p_ _e_ _a_ _t_
2 You speak like this when you speak loudly.   s _ _ _ _
3 If you talk about something, say if it is right or wrong and give your opinion, you do this. d _ _ _ _ _ _
4 When people talk angrily to each other because they don't agree, they do this. a _ _ _ _
5 Good friends do this when they meet. c _ _ _
6 If we don't understand, our teachers do this. e _ _ _ _ _ _
7 To say what something looks like. d _ _ _ _ _ _ _
8 If you change someone's opinion by talking to them, you do this. p _ _ _ _ _ _

1b Complete these conversations with the verbs in Exercise 1a.

1 **Teacher:** Does everyone understand?
  Girl: No, sorry. I wasn't listening. Can you ....repeat........ the instructions, please?

2 **Brother:** Dad, I was watching the TV before Sara came home.
  Sister: No, you weren't. I was!
  Father: Don't .... or I'll turn the TV off.

3 **Boy:** I can't do my Science homework. It's too difficult.
  Girl: Don't worry. I'll .... it to you.

4 **Girl:** Jon! Jon! I'm over here!
  Woman: Don't ....! He can hear you.

5 **Boy:** I've lost my bag. Have you seen it?
  Teacher: Can you .... your bag? When did you lose it?

6 **Girl:** Mum, it's raining. Can you give us a lift to school, please?
  Mum: I'm sorry, I'm busy. See if you can .... Dad to drive you.

7 **Boy:** Do you use your phone very much?
  Girl: Well, I often use it to .... to my friends at the weekends.

8 **Teacher:** Please get into small groups and .... the first question.
  Boy: Shall I start? I think phones are a good thing.

-ed / -ing adjectives

2 Exam candidates often make mistakes with -ed and -ing adjectives. Correct the mistakes in each of these sentences.

1 I was ~~surprise~~ to see my cousin at the party.
  ....surprised.........

2 I didn't enjoy the film. It was bored.
  ....

3 I'm very worry because I've got an exam tomorrow.
  ....

4 If you are interesting in the concert, please call me.
  ....

5 We're very exciting about your visit to our country.
  ....

6 When I am boring, I call my friends.
  ....

Reading Part 4

Exam advice

Look at the title and any photos first because these will help you understand the text.

1 For each question, choose the correct answer.

What do you know about sign language?

Around 5% of people in the world can't hear or can't hear very well, so how do they (1) .... to each other? They (2) .... their hands, face and body to have a conversation. Did you also know that there are many different (3) .... of sign languages? English is spoken in Britain, the USA and Australia but British, American and Australian sign language are not the same.

It is quite easy to (4) .... yourself sign language. Look online and you'll (5) .... hundreds of video lessons. You can even download an app on your phone.

It isn't clear when people first started using sign language. However, most people (6) .... that the first sign language dictionary was written in 1620.

1	**A** say	**B** talk	**C** tell
2	**A** use	**B** make	**C** give
3	**A** things	**B** kinds	**C** ways
4	**A** learn	**B** study	**C** teach
5	**A** find	**B** look	**C** meet
6	**A** decide	**B** hope	**C** agree

Grammar
The passive

1 Circle the correct form of the verbs.

The internet (1) *is used* / *was used* by over four billion people – that's over 50% of the world's population. Many of these people are members of social networks. The first social network site (2) *is started* / *was started* in 1997. It (3) *is called* / *was called* Six Degrees and it (4) *is used* / *was used* by about one million members. Many new friends (5) *are made* / *were made* on this site. Now Facebook (6) *is looked* / *was looked* at by millions every day! In 2010, photos (7) *are shared* / *were shared* for the first time on social networks. Nowadays, photos and videos (8) *are shared* / *were shared* on all sorts of sites and famous people (9) *are followed* / *were followed* by millions of people.

2 Complete this text with the present or past passive form of the verb in brackets.

GRAFFITI

Graffiti **(1)** ......is found...... (find) all over the world. The first examples of modern graffiti **(2)** .... (paint) in Philadelphia in the 1960s. One of the first artists **(3)** .... (call) Darryl McCray but he **(4)** .... (know) as 'Cornbread' too. Now graffiti **(5)** .... (use) by people to share opinions, show their art or even to say that they live in a place. New graffiti artists **(6)** .... (give) the name 'toys' and those with experience **(7)** .... (call) 'kings' or 'queens'. Graffiti has become very popular and it **(8)** .... (show) in many art museums. The free Urban Nation museum in Berlin is a great place to visit if you like graffiti. It **(9)** .... (build) in 2017 to show street art from all over the world.

3 Write complete answers to these questions. Use the present and the past passive and the words in brackets.

1 Who was the Mona Lisa painted by? (Leonardo da Vinci)
   The Mona Lisa was painted by Leonardo da Vinci.

2 Where is Irish spoken? (Ireland)
   ....

3 When was the first bike ridden? (1817)
   ....

4 What are footballs made of? (leather)
   ....

5 When was the first email sent? (1971)
   ....

6 Where are Samsung phones made? (South Korea)
   ....

Present perfect with *just, already* and *yet*

4 **Complete these sentences using the present perfect form of the verbs in the box and *just*.**

break go have miss ~~run~~ send

1 I'm tired because ....I've just run.... a race.
2 You're going to be late. You .... the bus.
3 Shh! Be quiet! Grandma and grandad .... to bed.
4 We can't eat anything else. We .... a big lunch.
5 Laura's coming. She .... me a message.
6 Liam isn't at school this week. He .... his leg.

5 **Complete this conversation with *already* or *yet*.**

Mum: Have you done your homework (1) ....yet.... ?
John: No, I haven't taken off my coat (2) ....
Mum: It's your cousin's birthday. Have you called her (3) .... ?
John: I've (4) .... sent her a message. Do I have to phone her?
Mum: No, not really. Have you got her a present (5) .... ?
John: Oh yes. I've (6) .... bought her a great book about photography.

6 **Look at the picture and write complete sentences. Use the present perfect with *just*, *already* or *yet*.**

1 (film / start)
....The film has already started.....
2 (a man / get off a bus)
....
3 (six people / sit down in the cinema)
....
4 (two girls / arrive)
....
5 (they / close the door)
....

Reading Part 5

Try to write a word in each space even if you are uncertain about the answer.

Exam advice

1 **For each question, write the correct answer.**

Write ONE word for each gap.

From: Simon
To: Guy

Thanks (0) ....for.... your last email. I'm sorry I haven't written before but I (1) .... just returned from a Spanish course in Granada, Spain. I travelled there (2) .... plane and I stayed with a really friendly family. There were two children. Elena was older (3) .... me but Diego was the same age.

(4) .... the morning I had lessons in a school. On the first day, I (5) .... given a test. They put me in the beginner's class because I didn't know (6) .... to speak Spanish, but after three weeks I knew a lot!

See you soon,

Simon

14 Vocabulary extra

Communication verbs and adjectives

1 Read what these people are saying. Then match 1–10 with the verbs in the box.

answer	......9......	describe	....
argue	....	discuss	....
ask	....	repeat	....
chat	....	shout	....
cry	....	suggest	....

1 'Shall I say that again?'

2 'I don't agree. What do you think?'

3 'Why don't we watch a film?'

4 'Come here now!'

5 'I can't find my teddy!'

6 'What? I never said that!'

7 'He's tall with short brown hair and glasses.'

8 'What do we have to do now?'

9 'That's an easy question! 7 x 2 is 14.'

10 'Jack's party was cool and then we...'

2 Read the description and write the adjective. Use the words in the box.

> brave   clever   ~~famous~~   friendly
> funny   kind   noisy   quiet

1 Everyone has heard of Shakira. She's ...*famous*... .
2 I often laugh when I'm with my cousin. He's ....
3 He's a lovely person who helps other people. He's ....
4 Your cousin shouts a lot. He's very ....
5 We always do well at school. We're ....
6 My neighbour always says hello. She's ....
7 I never speak when I'm studying. I'm ....
8 She's not afraid of insects. She's ....

3 Circle the correct words to complete these sentences.

1 We were (surprised) / surprising to see Max at the party. He doesn't like parties.
2 My best friend is interested / interesting in football.
3 I enjoyed the play. The acting was amazed / amazing.
4 I've got some excited / exciting news. I've just won first prize in a sailing competition.
5 We walked through a forest, then climbed a mountain. I was very tired / tiring at the end.
6 I love rugby but my friends think it's bored / boring.

4 Complete these sentences with at, in, on, from or for.

1 I watched a film ......*at*...... home last night.
2 Everest is the highest mountain .... the world.
3 I love skateboarding .... the weekend.
4 Thank you .... coming to my party.
5 Hurry! The bus leaves .... ten minutes.
6 I'm free every day .... 5 pm to 8 pm.

Keep in touch!   59

Acknowledgements

The authors and publishers acknowledge the following sources of copyright material and are grateful for the permissions granted. While every effort has been made, it has not always been possible to identify the sources of all the material used, or to trace all copyright holders. If any omissions are brought to our notice, we will be happy to include the appropriate acknowledgements on reprinting and in the next update to the digital edition, as applicable.

Key: U = Unit

Photography

The following images are sourced from Getty Images.

U1: JGI/Jamie Grill/Blend Images; Mark Edward Atkinson/Blend Images; Flashpop/DigitalVision; Layland Masuda/Moment Open; **U2**: Paul Bradbury/OJO Images; **U3**: Trinette Reed/Blend Images; **U4**: Rob Lewine; martin-dm/E+; **U5**: fotokostic/iStock/Getty Images Plus; Hero Images; **U6**: Radius Images/Getty Images Plus; monkeybusinessimages/iStock/Getty Images Plus; Moxie Productions/Blend Images; artparadigm/DigitalVision; Plattform; majana/iStock/Getty Images Plus; Peathegee Inc/Blend Images; **U7**: Peter Adams/Photolibrary; **U8**: Frederick M. Brown/Getty Images Entertainment; **U9**: Jena Ardell/Moment; Hero Images; **U10**: Westend61; VikramRaghuvanshi/iStock/Getty Images Plus; PaoloBis/Moment; **U11**: Dougal Waters/The Image Bank; FGorgun/iStock/Getty Images Plus; Martin Sundberg/UpperCut Images; Uwe Umstatter/Radius Images; **U13**: altrendo images/Stockbyte; Maskot; Daisy-Daisy/iStock/Getty Images Plus; Imgorthand/E+; **U14**: Phoenixns/iStock/Getty Images Plus.

The following photographs have been sourced from other sources.
U8: Courtesy of Aksel Rykkvin/John Andresen; Courtesy of djarchjnr.

Front cover photography by Hans Neleman/The Image Bank/Getty Images; Thissatan/iStock/Getty Images Plus/Getty Images.

Illustrations

Jorge Santillan, Martyn Cain; Abel Ippolito, Laszlo Veres

Audio

Produced by Leon Chambers and recorded at The SoundHouse Studios, London

Page make up

Wild Apple Design Ltd